THE IMPORTANCE OF

Queen Victoria

These and other titles are included in The Importance
Of biography series:

Alexander the Great	Harry Houdini
Muhammad Ali	Thomas Jefferson
Louis Armstrong	Mother Jones
Clara Barton	Chief Joseph
Napoleon Bonaparte	Malcolm X
Rachel Carson	Margaret Mead
Charlie Chaplin	Michelangelo
Cesar Chavez	Wolfgang Amadeus Mozart
Winston Churchill	John Muir
Cleopatra	Sir Isaac Newton
Christopher Columbus	Richard M. Nixon
Hernando Cortes	Georgia O'Keeffe
Marie Curie	Louis Pasteur
Amelia Earhart	Pablo Picasso
Thomas Edison	Jackie Robinson
Albert Einstein	Anwar Sadat
Duke Ellington	Margaret Sanger
Dian Fossey	Oskar Schindler
Benjamin Franklin	John Steinbeck
Galileo Galilei	Jim Thorpe
Martha Graham	Mark Twain
Stephen Hawking	Queen Victoria
Jim Henson	Pancho Villa
Adolf Hitler	H. G. Wells

THE IMPORTANCE OF

Queen Victoria

by
Patricia D. Netzley

Lucent Books, P.O. Box 289011, San Diego, CA 92198-9011

Library of Congress Cataloging-in-Publication Data

Netzley, Patricia D.
    The importance of Queen Victoria / by Patricia D. Netzley.
        p.   cm.
    Includes bibliographical references (p.   ) and index.
    Summary: Discusses the importance in history of the
queen who ruled England for sixty-four years and during
whose reign Great Britain expanded its influence throughout the world.
    ISBN 1-56006-063-8 (lib. : alk. paper)
    1. Victoria, Queen of Great Britain, 1819–1901—Juvenile
literature.   2. Great Britain—History—Victoria, 1837–1901—
Juvenile literature.   3. Queens—Great Britain—Biography—
Juvenile literature.   [1. Victoria, Queen of Great Britain,
1819–1901.   2. Great Britain—History—Victoria, 1837–1901.
3. Kings, queens, rulers, etc.]   I. Title.
DA557.N48   1996
941.081'092—dc20   95–43123
[B]   CIP
                                                        AC

The author wishes to thank Ray Netzley, George and Marge Faber, Mike Faber, and Eleanor Morgan for their help and support during the preparation of this book.

Contents

Foreword

THE IMPORTANCE OF biography series deals with individuals who have made a unique contribution to history. The editors of the series have deliberately chosen to cast a wide net and include people from all fields of endeavor. Individuals from politics, music, art, literature, philosophy, science, sports, and religion are all represented. In addition, the editors did not restrict the series to individuals whose accomplishments have helped change the course of history. Of necessity, this criterion would have eliminated many whose contribution was great, though limited. Charles Darwin, for example, was responsible for radically altering the scientific view of the natural history of the world. His achievements continue to impact the study of science today. Others, such as Chief Joseph of the Nez Percé, played a pivotal role in the history of their own people. While Joseph's influence does not extend much beyond the Nez Percé, his nonviolent resistance to white expansion and his continuing role in protecting his tribe and his homeland remain an inspiration to all.

These biographies are more than factual chronicles. Each volume attempts to emphasize an individual's contributions both in his or her own time and for posterity. For example, the voyages of Christopher Columbus opened the way to European colonization of the New World. Unquestionably, his encounter with the New World brought monumental changes to both Europe and the Americas in his day. Today, however, the broader impact of Columbus's voyages is being critically scrutinized. *Christopher Columbus,* as well as every biography in The Importance Of series, includes and evaluates the most recent scholarship available on each subject.

Each author includes a wide variety of primary and secondary source quotations to document and substantiate his or her work. All quotes are footnoted to show readers exactly how and where biographers derive their information, as well as provide stepping stones to further research. These quotations enliven the text by giving readers eyewitness views of the life and times of each individual covered in The Importance Of series.

Finally, each volume is enhanced by photographs, bibliographies, chronologies, and comprehensive indexes. For both the casual reader and the student engaged in research, The Importance Of biographies will be a fascinating adventure into the lives of people who have helped shape humanity's past and present, and who will continue to shape its future.

IMPORTANT DATES IN THE LIFE OF QUEEN VICTORIA

1819
Born in England on May 24; christened Alexandrina Victoria

1820
Duke of Kent dies; King George III dies; George IV ascends the throne

1824
Lehzen becomes her governess

1830
King George IV dies; William IV ascends the throne

1832
Begins keeping a journal

1837
King William IV dies on June 20, and Victoria assumes the throne; accepts Melbourne as her prime minister

1838
Coronation on June 28

1839
Fights with Robert Peel over her ladies-of-the-bedchamber; Lady Flora Hastings dies

1840
Marries Prince Albert of Coburg on February 10; first attempt on the queen's life occurs on June 10; gives birth to first child, the Princess Royal ("Vicky"), on November 21

1841
Gives birth to the Prince of Wales, Albert Edward ("Bertie"), November 9; Peel becomes prime minister

1842
First ride on a train; target of more assassination attempts

1843
Buys royal residence at Osbourne; Princess Alice born on April 25

1844
Prince Alfred born on August 6

1846
Attacks Palmerston for blunder regarding Spanish marriages; Princess Helena born on May 25

1848
Princess Louise born on March 18; visits Balmoral Castle for the first time

1850
Prince Arthur born on May 1

1851
Prince Albert's Great Exhibition; employs John Brown as groom

1853
Receives chloroform and gives birth to Prince Leopold on April 7

1854
Crimean War begins

1857
Hands out first Victoria Crosses; Princess Beatrice born on April 14

1858
Attends Princess Vicky's wedding; Great Britain takes over government of India

1861
Duchess of Kent dies; Prince Albert dies

1863
Argues for neutrality in war between Denmark and Prussia; attends wedding of Prince Albert Edward

1865
John Brown becomes "The Queen's Highland Servant"

1868
Publishes *Leaves from the Journal of My Life in the Highlands;* Disraeli becomes prime minister, then Gladstone becomes prime minister

1874
Asks for law restricting public worship practices; Disraeli becomes prime minister again

1876
Royal Titles Act passed in Parliament declaring her empress of India

1880
Gladstone becomes prime minister again

1881
Disraeli dies

1883
John Brown dies

1884
Publishes *More Leaves from a Journal of My Life in the Highlands;* helps establish Royal Commission on Housing

1887
Celebrates Golden Jubilee; employs Abdul Karim ("Munshi")

1897
Celebrates Diamond Jubilee

1899
Boer War begins in South Africa; Victoria's eightieth birthday

1901
Dies at Osbourne House on January 22

An Anchor in Rough and Stormy Seas

Cannons boomed as the royal yacht *Alberta* pulled away from the town of Cowes on the Isle of Wight. Usually its passage to England was pleasant, but today the mood onboard was as somber as the gray sky overhead. It was February 1, 1901, and the ship carried the body of Great Britain's ruler, Queen Victoria. She had died while staying at her island residence, Osbourne House. Now she was going to her final resting place, a mausoleum at Frogmore, near Windsor Castle outside of London.

Slowly the *Alberta* sailed between two long, stationary rows of warships. The warships' hulls were painted black in mourning, and each one fired its guns as the queen's yacht passed. Behind the *Alberta* sailed the *Victoria and Albert*, carrying Britain's new king, Edward VII, who was Victoria's eldest son. The ship was followed by the imperial yacht of Kaiser Wilhelm II of Germany, who was the late queen's grandson.

The Most Beloved Queen

The procession docked at Portsmouth, England, to the strains of Chopin's Funeral March. Hundreds of people waited onshore to pay their respects to Her Royal

Hundreds of people pay their respects as Queen Victoria's funeral procession passes by in 1901. The beloved queen would be remembered for bringing a sense of order to England during its entry into the modern age.

Majesty, perhaps the most beloved queen that England had ever known.

By now not only all of Great Britain but much of the world was in mourning. The queen's death had come as a surprise, even though she had been eighty-one years old and bedridden for weeks, after suffering a series of small strokes. Still, when she died on January 22, 1901, with all her children and grandchildren at her side, "It seemed as though the keystone had fallen out of the arch of Heaven," according to poet Robert Bridges.[1] The poet Ford Madox Ford wrote it was "A shock,/ A change in the beat of the clock."[2] Newspapers reported that people in the streets were "dim figures wandering aimlessly here and there without a word spoken."[3] Peasants said prayers for her. Street sweepers draped their brooms in black crepe to mark her passing.

Queen Victoria had ruled England for sixty-four years. During her reign, Great Britain had expanded its influence throughout the world, adding such places as India, Burma, New Zealand, and Hong Kong to the list of countries under its control. At the same time, wars and revolutions were occurring in other nations. The American Civil War, the Spanish-American War, the Sino-Japanese War, and the overthrow of the French government by Emperor Napoleon III all happened during Victoria's lifetime, as did the assassinations of two U.S. presidents, Abraham Lincoln and James Garfield.

A White Funeral

In contrast, Victoria's realm was stable and strong. The queen was a steady fixture in the lives of her people. Despite sweeping advances in technology, she remained firmly committed to traditional beliefs and values. Victoria lived through the invention of photography, pasteurization, the telegraph and telephone, the phono-

Victoria, pictured with two of her children, was a devoted and caring mother of nine. Through their marriages, her children and grandchildren would eventually wear many of the crowns of Europe.

graph, the typewriter, the electric light and electric car, the steam engine, the gas burner, the bicycle, the sewing machine and paper dress patterns, dynamite, ice machines, the canning process for fruits and vegetables, and many, many other discoveries that drastically affected modern life. Yet she did not allow material possessions to become more important than human beings.

She was devoted to her family. Through her own marriage and the eventual marriages of her nine children, she established familial relationships with the rulers of Russia, Germany, Greece, Denmark, and Romania. Her influence was extensive. Her heirs would have an impact on world events for years to come.

She was a loving, concerned mother, and none grieved her death more than

Full of Contradictions

In her book Victoria R.I.*, Elizabeth Longford comments on Victoria's personality.*

"It is difficult to convey the richness of her contradictions. She was both brave and nervous. So greatly did she fear the sea that though born a good sailor she became a very bad one; the Empress Eugenie had to assure her that 'Queens are not drowned.' She was afraid of sports, from ice hockey to hunting. When her son-in-law, Prince Christian, lost his eye in a gun accident she wrote: 'my dislike & fear of shooting will only increase.' She was so terrified of railway accidents that she never . . . [allowed her train to travel] at more than 50 miles an hour. . . .

In human relations she was both unselfish and inconsiderate, tactful and blunt, sympathetic and hard, patient and fidgety, direct and devious, irresistibly charming and bristling with 'repellent power.' While receiving her at a library the librarian seized the opportunity to make an introduction:

'Your Majesty, this is my daughter.'

'I came to see the library.'

Majesty swept on."

---

her children. "No one knows what the daily missing of [my mother's] tender care and love is to me," her youngest daughter, Princess Beatrice, wrote. ". . . my heart is indeed left utterly desolate."[4] The Queen's eldest daughter, also named Victoria but called Vicky, wrote on a tear-stained page of her diary, "Oh, how can my pen write it, my sweet darling beloved Mama; the best of mothers and greatest of Queens, our centre and help and support—all seems a blank, a terrible awful dream. Realise it one cannot."[5]

Still, Victoria's family had to be strong, for they had many specific duties to perform. The queen had left behind strict instructions about her funeral. In accordance with her wishes, her family dressed her all in white and placed her in a white coffin. They draped her wedding veil across her face and placed a silver crucifix in her hands. Beside her they tucked the dressing gown of her late husband, Prince Albert, as well as a plaster cast of his hand and some family photographs. Then they sprinkled the queen's body with spring flowers, closed her coffin, and had it carried to Osbourne's chapel, which they filled with strongly scented white gardenias.

For its sea journey ten days later, the coffin was covered with white and gold cloth embroidered with a cross and the royal coat of arms. Then at Portsmouth, England, the queen's coffin was carried to a special, private train bound for London's Victoria Station. Along the route people knelt beside the train tracks and bowed their heads.

The coffin was taken by carriage from Victoria Station to Paddington Station, where another train waited to take the queen to Windsor. The streets in Windsor were decorated, not in black, but in purple cashmere with white satin bows, because Queen Victoria had specifically ordered that her military funeral be bright. She wanted uniforms to be white and gold, horses to be white. She wanted musicians to play Chopin, Beethoven, and Highland laments rather than the traditional sad drumroll of Handel's Funeral March. And she wanted the royal standard to fly from the gun carriages that bore her coffin from place to place.

A Dreaded Mishap

Despite the queen's careful instructions, things still went wrong. As her carriage

During her sixty-four-year reign, Victoria was instrumental in expanding Great Britain's influence throughout the world.

was leaving Windsor Station, the horses shied and snapped their traces—something Victoria had feared. "I would wish just to say that as a gun carriage is very rough jolting and noisy," she had written in her will, "one ought to be properly arranged."[6]

For a moment no one knew what to do. Then a group of sailors led by a noted admiral unharnessed all the horses. Using a length of cord, the men pulled the carriage themselves—uphill and to the beat of drums.

King Edward VII and Kaiser Wilhelm II rode behind the coffin. They were accompanied by Victoria's cousin George, the duke of Cambridge. George had once been the queen's commander in chief, and his presence added to the military nature of her funeral. The next member of the procession was also a famous military hero, the general and earl Sir Frederick Roberts. Roberts was followed by the closed carriages of Victoria's grief-stricken daughters. One woman who witnessed the passage of the procession later commented that she was "impressed by the silence of the streets, the absence of music, the continuous booming of the guns that had almost a fateful sound, then the noise of the horses' hoofs striking the road, the rattle of swords, and the clatter of the stirrups."[7] A total of eighty-one guns, one for each year of the queen's life, thundered out their tribute.

With Albert at Last

Finally the procession reached St. George's Chapel at Windsor Castle, where a short service was held. Afterwards the queen's coffin was placed in the Albert Memorial Chapel, and on the morning of February 4 it was taken to the mausoleum at Frogmore. Over its doors were these words: "*Vale desideratissime.* Farewell most beloved. Here at length I shall rest with thee, with thee in Christ I shall rise again."[8] They were addressed to Queen Victoria's beloved husband, Prince Albert.

Thirty-six years before, she had made arrangements to lie in a sarcophagus beside his. At that time she remarked in her journal, "Oh! could I but be there soon!"[9] In forty years of widowhood, she had never recovered from Albert's death. Under the domes of the mausoleum she had ordered inscribed:

> Lay her beneath the shade
> Of Windsor's Royal towers
> Where in sad widowed hours
> Her tomb she made.[10]

And as a part of her funeral service she included the hymn:

> Life's dream is past,
> All its sin, its sadness.
> Brightly at last
> Dawns a day of gladness.[11]

Today the two sarcophagi rest side by side, each with its own marble statue on top. The figure of Prince Albert, accurate to the finest detail, looks heavenward, while that of Queen Victoria shows her face inclined slightly toward her husband.

A Sustaining Symbol

Immediately after the queen's funeral, King Edward VII began changing everything around him. He got rid of many of his mother's possessions, renovated the royal residences, and turned Osbourne House over to Great Britain for use as a naval convalescent hospital and college, despite specific instructions in Victoria's will that the home remain in the family. Edward then began conducting royal hunts and other festive activities. He was a lively, boisterous individual, in stark contrast to his stately and very proper predecessor.

Consequently, many Britons were uncomfortable with their new monarch. Author Henry James said:

> I mourn the safe and motherly old middle-class queen, who held the nation warm under the fold of her big, hideous Scotch-plaid shawl and whose duration had been so extraordinarily convenient and beneficent. I felt her death much more than I should have expected; she was a sustaining symbol.[12]

Victoria, a symbol of virtue and tradition, brought dignity back to the royal monarchy.

Modern Inventions

As Elizabeth Longford explains in her book Victoria R.I., *Victoria embraced modern technology.*

"[Queen Victoria] appreciated new amenities. Though she said that 'negotiating by telegraph is a dreadful business,' she made full use of it and the Princess of Wales complained that the telephone between [the two of their homes] never stopped ringing. She was reported to have fallen for the tricycle in 1881 and even to have gone for a spin. Electric light was one of the few inventions she did not praise; it either hurt her eyes or was not bright enough."

During her reign from 1837 to 1901, Queen Victoria represented virtue and tradition. According to the queen's godson, author Victor Mallet:

The late Victorian age was one of wealth and low taxation, [but] it was also one of shocking poverty, of class distinctions, much snobbery and much servility. In compensation, life was less of a rush, leaving more time for thoughtfulness and things in nature and the arts. The Queen and her rather dowdy Court set the example for virtuous lives. Routine was eternal: change almost unthinkable. [13]

Unlike previous British rulers, such as Kings George III and IV, who behaved rudely and immorally without concern for public opinion, Victoria cared about what people thought of her. Because of this she probably kept the monarchy from being overthrown entirely. According to biographer Stanley Weintraub:

What Victoria had left behind as legacy was the sturdy ceremonial monarchy now ratified by public affection, by a yearning for continuity and tradition, and by the middle-class values that were her own and that remain beneath the fairy-tale veneer of royalty. She became England. [14]

And so Queen Victoria was important not just for the accomplishments of her realm but for the steadiness she provided to the world. Amidst drastic changes in technology, science, medicine, politics, and almost every other aspect of life at the dawn of the modern age, Victoria remained a person of unchanging values and beliefs. In some cases this stubbornness exasperated those around her. Certainly her children had cause for complaint, for Victoria made her opinions about everything well known to them. Yet they recognized that she also provided them—and the world—with a needed anchor in a time of rough and difficult seas.

1 An Unhappy Childhood

Princess Victoria's birth on May 24, 1819, was not marked with great importance, because no one expected her to become queen. After all, there were so many people ahead of her in the line of succession for the British throne. When King George III died, the eldest of his seven sons, Prince George, would rule. When George IV died, the responsibility would pass to George III's second son, Frederick. When Frederick died, George III's third son, William IV, would become king. William had recently married. If he had any children, they would wear the crown after his death. Otherwise it would be handed to George III's fourth son, Edward, also known as the duke of Kent. Edward was Victoria's father. Only after his death would she become queen.

A Father's Faith

Even though the odds were against it, Edward believed that his little princess would someday rule England. Long ago, a Gypsy fortune teller had told him that he would have a daughter who would be a great queen. He had so much confidence in this prediction that when his wife, the German princess Victoire of Leiningen, was about to give birth, he decided to move her from their home in Europe all the way to England, a journey of 427 miles, so the baby could be born there.

He believed that his people would not accept a ruler who had been born outside of Great Britain. "The time may come,"

Victoria's father, the duke of Kent, believed from the beginning that his daughter would eventually inherit the British throne.

Kensington Palace, the birthplace of Victoria. The duke, knowing that British citizens would be unlikely to accept a foreign-born ruler, moved to England with his pregnant wife so Victoria could be born there.

Edward said, "when legitimacy may be challenged, and challenged with effect, from the circumstance of the birth taking place on foreign soil."[15]

But the duke of Kent didn't have enough money to pay for a trip to England. He needed help from his family. By this time his father was mentally ill, so he wrote to his oldest brother asking for a loan. Prince George's reply was cold. He refused to help Edward bring his pregnant wife to England.

Prince George had always disliked Edward, and he couldn't imagine his brother's child sitting on the throne. He was also upset that his own daughter, Princess Charlotte, would never have the chance to become queen. Just two years earlier, Charlotte, who was married to the duchess of Kent's brother Leopold, had died after giving birth to a stillborn son.

The prince hoped that Edward would have to stay in Europe. However, Edward found friends who loaned him enough money for the trip. Soon he and his wife reached London. They stayed at Kensington Palace, where their baby was born in the presence of the duke of Wellington, the archbishop of Canterbury, the bishop of London, the Chancellor of the Exchequer, and other important witnesses. Edward wanted no one to question that this child was indeed his daughter, "a pretty little Princess, as plump as a partridge."[16]

Prince George hated Edward all the more after he became the father of a healthy baby girl. George ignored his brother at official ceremonies and refused to help the duke with his debts, which were mounting rapidly.

Edward had been living beyond his means for years. He began borrowing money when he was seventeen years old. At that time, he was in Germany undergoing military training, and he believed that his parents were sending him insufficient

In this quote from Monica Charlot's biography, Victoria: The Young Queen, *Feodora writes to congratulate her half sister Victoria on her tenth birthday.*

"If I had wings and could fly like a bird I should fly in at your window like the little robin to-day, and wish you many very happy returns on the 24th and tell you how I love you, dearest sister, and how often I think of you and long to see you. I think if I were once with you again I could not leave you so soon. I should wish to stay with you, and what would poor Ernest [her husband] say if I were to leave him so long? He would perhaps try to fly after me, but I fear he would not get far; he is rather tall and heavy for flying."

funds to maintain the lifestyle necessary for him to distinguish himself from the other trainees. He wanted to appear royal no matter how much it cost. Later, to outfit himself for various military campaigns, he bought expensive dishes, furniture, clothing, books, and wine, much of which was captured by the enemy and had to be replaced. When he married the duchess of Kent, he had a lavish wedding ceremony and showered his bride with jewelry, clothing, horses, and other costly gifts.

He wanted the christening of his first child to be equally lavish. But Prince George insisted the ceremony be simple and private. George had been named regent, or acting sovereign, because of the king's failing mind, and made all decisions regarding the royal family. Edward argued that future heirs to the British throne were always christened at public, formal events, yet Prince George couldn't be swayed.

Nor would George allow the duke of Kent to choose his own daughter's name.

George said the girl could not be called Elizabeth, after Queen Elizabeth I, or Charlotte, after the deceased princess. And he would certainly not permit the feminine version of his own name, Georgiana. He also turned down the name Augusta, after Edward's mother-in-law, saying it was too majestic—after all, one of Prince George's brothers was named Augustus. In the end George ordered the presiding archbishop of Canterbury to christen his brother's baby Alexandrina, after the emperor of Russia. Her middle name would be Victoria, after her mother. Edward was angry that his daughter had not been given a name from British royalty.

Poor Treatment

In the months that followed, Prince George continued to treat Edward with contempt. He remained convinced that Princess Victoria would never ascend to the throne and didn't see any reason to favor her.

He refused to help the duke of Kent support his family or pay his debts. In an effort to reduce his expenses, Edward decided to leave London. He rented a modest house near the sea at Sidmouth and moved his family there. His wife, the duchess of Kent, had two children by a previous marriage. Her young daughter, thirteen-year-old Feodora, lived with the family. Her other child, Charles, was away at school in Switzerland.

Shortly after Edward and his family arrived in Sidmouth, both Victoria, just eight months old, and her father, then fifty-two, came down with terrible colds. While the duchess nursed the infant, the duke decided to treat his illness with brisk walks despite the bitter weather. Soon he complained of a fever and took to his bed. On January 23, 1820, he died of pneumonia. Six days later King George III died. Prince George was the new King George IV, and Princess Victoria was now third in line for the throne, after her uncles Frederick and William.

King George IV did not pity the fatherless princess. He refused to give any money towards the one-year-old girl's support, hoping that her mother's poverty would force her to leave the British seashore and take the child back to Germany. He wanted Victoria out of England. "It was wonderful how George IV was bent on this idea," recalled Victoria's uncle King Leopold, some years later, "and in those days the wish and will of the head of the state was still a very serious concern and the people very subservient to it."[17]

To reduce his overwhelming debt, Edward moved his family outside of London to a more affordable house in Sidmouth. A few months later Edward died, leaving young Victoria and her mother in poverty.

After the duke of Kent's death, King George IV (pictured) allowed Victoria and the duchess of Kent to move back to Kensington Palace, though he refused to help them financially.

The penniless duchess was about to do as the king wished and leave England when her brother intervened. Leopold insisted that King George allow Victoria and her mother to return to London. He said they should live permanently in Kensington Palace, where Victoria would learn to speak English instead of German, the only language the duchess knew.

Normally the king of England refused to listen to anyone else's demands, but he did not want to oppose his former son-in-law. Leopold was well liked by the British people. The public sympathized with his grief over the death of Princess Charlotte,

whom they too had loved. Not wishing to anger his subjects, King George decided to allow the duchess and her baby to move into Kensington Palace, although he still refused to help them financially. After all, the king said, Victoria's Uncle Leopold was certainly "rich enough to take care of her."[18]

Hard Times

Leopold did agree to pay for Princess Victoria's upbringing and eventual education, but not for her mother's household expenses, nor for the debts the duke had incurred during his lifetime. These would have to be paid off by the duchess herself. She had received some insurance money upon her husband's death and also received a meager allowance from the British government. The duchess hoped this allowance would be increased, but the members of Parliament refused, saying it was unnecessary to support the duchess because Leopold was already giving money to the family.

The Duchess was in despair. For advice she turned to Captain John Conroy, who had served her late husband. According to the duchess, Conroy had acted "as a dear devoted friend of my Edward, and does not desert his widow, doing all he can by dealing with my affairs. . . . His energy and capability are wonderful."[19]

But Conroy didn't handle the duchess of Kent's finances any better than her husband had. The debts mounted higher and higher, especially after the duchess took out a loan to repair Kensington Palace, which was drafty and damp.

And so Princess Victoria lived amidst great poverty. She slept on a cot in her mother's bedroom and had no privacy, even as she grew from an infant to a young girl and then a teenager. "I never had a room to myself," she wrote years later. "I never had a sofa, nor an easy chair; and there was not a single carpet that was not threadbare."[20]

Victoria described the sparse household of her youth.

We lived in a very simple, plain manner. Breakfast was at half past eight, luncheon at half past one, dinner at seven—to which I came generally (when it was no regular large dinner party)—eating my bread and milk out of a small silver basin. Tea was only allowed as a great treat in later years.[21]

Not only that, but the duchess had "not a spoon or napkin of her own, as everything belonged to the creditors,"[22] wrote Leopold.

Princess Mary, George IV's sister, did not believe that an heir to the throne should live in such poverty. When Victoria was still only a year old, Mary wrote to tell the king "of the deplorable reduced state the unfortunate Dss. of Kent is left in— and some little immediate assistance I plead is necessary."[23] King George would not yield.

He was still convinced that Victoria would never rule England for two reasons. First, she was only a baby and might not live to adulthood. Second, Prince William and his young wife Adelaide had just given birth to their own little girl, Elizabeth Georgina Adelaide. This child, whom the British people called "little Queen Bess," had taken Victoria's place in the order of succession, and King George expected William and Adelaide to produce even more heirs.

But at three months of age, Elizabeth went into convulsions and died. Then, a few months later, Adelaide miscarried twins. Although she was only thirty, Adelaide knew she would never bear a future king or queen of England.

"My children are dead," Adelaide wrote to Victoria's mother," but your child lives and she is mine too."[24]

A Change in Fortune

Victoria's Aunt Adelaide and Uncle William treated her with great kindness. "My dear little heart," Adelaide wrote to her on one occasion, "I hope you are well and don't forget Aunt Adelaide, who loves you so fondly. . . . God bless and preserve you is the constant prayer of your most truly affectionate Aunt, Adelaide."[25]

Victoria's nursemaids and her beloved half sister Feodora also treated the little girl well—too well, according to her mother, who thought they spoiled her. According to the duchess, from the time Victoria was a year old she showed "symptoms of wanting to get her own way."[26] When she was five, her new governess, Fraulein Louise Lehzen, found her to be the most "passionate and naughty"[27] child she had ever seen. The girl refused to learn her letters, and Lehzen decided to be firm with her. Victoria responded on one occasion by throwing a pair of scissors at her governess.

The princess displayed her temper to others, too. For instance, she shouted at her piano teacher and banged down the lid of her piano. But through Lehzen's firm guidance she eventually learned how to behave. "I adored her," Victoria later

Victoria's sketch of her governess, Louise Lehzen. Lehzen, who called the young princess the most "passionate and naughty" child she had ever seen, was hired to teach Victoria court etiquette.

said of her governess, "though I was greatly in awe of her."[28]

Under Lehzen's influence, the princess grew serious about her lessons. She finally learned to read, and she dutifully practiced her piano. At the age of eight she received several tutors and began studying arithmetic, history, religion, drawing, dancing, and riding. She learned French and German as well as English. Her lessons went from half past nine to half past eleven, after which she had playtime and mealtime, followed by lessons again from three to six, even on Saturdays. "This Lady [Victoria]," wrote Sir Walter Scott, "is educated with much care, and is watched so closely that

no busy maid has a moment to whisper 'You are heir of England.'"[29]

By now Victoria's position as heir had become much stronger. Her Uncle Frederick had died, so she was second in line for the throne. Many important British figures had begun to visit her at Kensington Palace.

King George had seen his niece only a few times, but on each occasion she had behaved beautifully. Once, when he invited her to tell an orchestra what she wanted them to play, she quickly replied, "God Save the King."[30] Now King George considered taking Victoria away from her mother so she could live at court. His advisor, the duke of Wellington, persuaded him to wait, but the possibility remained in the king's thoughts.

Victoria's Regent

Suspecting what the king had in mind, the duchess decided to keep her daughter away from court as much as possible. She didn't want to lose control of the future queen. In fact, she and John Conroy had devised a plan that would bring them power and wealth.

The duchess would have herself declared Victoria's regent. This meant that if Victoria became queen while she was still a child, the duchess—with Conroy's help—would make decisions for her. In this way the pair would be the true rulers of England.

But Conroy and the duchess knew that King George would never allow a regency. The king had always hated Victoria's mother. He thought her a stupid and annoying foreigner who didn't deserve to be

"Dear Sweet Little Dash"

Victoria loved dogs, and as biographer Elizabeth Longford explains in Victoria R.I., *the princess had a unique relationship with her first pet, a spaniel named Dash.*

"There was a moment when Sir John Conroy redeemed himself in Victoria's eyes. He presented her mother on January 14th, 1833, with a King Charles's spaniel called Dash. Three months later Princess Victoria had adopted 'DEAR SWEET LITTLE DASH' and was dressing him up in scarlet jacket and blue trousers. She gave him for Christmas three india-rubber balls and two bits of gingerbread decorated with holly and candles. Dash showed his devotion by jumping into the sea and swimming after her yacht; when she was ill he spent 'his little life' in her room."

Victoria had a lifelong love of animals, especially dogs.

"Her Dolls Were Her Friends"

Cecil Woodham-Smith describes Princess Victoria's devotion to her many dolls in her biography Queen Victoria.

"Her dolls were her friends, substitutes for the girl companions she was never allowed to have. . . . They were adult dolls . . . dressed by the Princess with the help of Lehzen. . . . They mainly represented characters from plays and operas seen by the Princess. They lived in a box and she kept a list of 132 of them mentioning the name of each and the character it was intended to represent. The dolls themselves had no magnificence, they were quite ordinary, from three to nine inches high with the 'Dutch doll' type of face, easy to pack away. The Princess found an outlet for her imagination and affection in dressing and playing with her dolls and they continued to be a favourite amusement until she was nearly 14."

Without any friends her own age, Victoria kept herself amused by playing with her large collection of dolls.

linked to the throne of England. Consequently, when George IV died on June 26, 1830, John Conroy was overjoyed.

Conroy believed that the newly crowned King William IV would be friendlier to the duchess. King William seemed to be a plain and simple man who wanted what was best for Victoria, now eleven. Surely Conroy and the duchess could convince him to do what they wanted.

2 The Power of the Throne

King William IV was indeed very different from his older brother. According to biographer Stanley Weintraub, while King George had kept to himself, King William

> enjoyed prying into the workings of his regime, reviewing the Guards, both horse and foot, and even inspecting the Tower of London [and was] a little, old, red-nosed, weather-beaten, jolly-looking person, with an ungraceful air and carriage.[31]

Another biographer, Giles St. Aubyn, noted that "the King was an eccentric, peppery, good-natured old sailor, while the Queen, who was twenty-eight years younger than her husband, had beautiful manners, a generous heart and a natural piety."[32]

King William and Queen Adelaide were both very popular with their subjects. Moreover, they truly loved Victoria and wanted to spend as much time with her as possible. But John Conroy didn't want that to happen. He wanted to be the only one who influenced the future queen of England.

He urged the duchess to write to King William asking that as Victoria's mother she be appointed regent and receive the title Dowager Princess of Wales. This title carried much prestige and would put the duchess on the same level with more important members of the royal family. In

William IV, crowned king in 1830, found himself at odds with Victoria's mother, who wished to keep her daughter away from the court.

her letter the duchess also insisted that as regent she would deserve an increase in her allowance. In addition, she wanted Victoria's allowance paid directly to her until the girl came of age at eighteen. The duchess still had many debts and felt that Kensington Palace was not lavish enough for the future queen of England.

A Most Solemn Event

"I felt that my confirmation was one of the most solemn and important events and acts in my life; and that I trusted that it might have a salutary effect on my mind. I felt deeply repentant for all that I had done which was wrong and trusted in God Almighty to strengthen my heart and mind; and to forsake all that is bad and follow all that is virtuous and right. I went with the firm determination to become a true Christian, to try and comfort my dear Mamma in all her griefs, trials, and anxieties, and to become a dutiful and affectionate daughter to her. Also to be obedient to *dear* Lehzen, who has done so much for me. I was dressed in a white lace dress, with a white crape bonnet with a wreath of white roses round it. I went in the chariot with my dear Mamma and the others followed in another carriage."

When King William did not reply to the letter, the duchess took her petition to Parliament. She knew that they would help her. Normally, the regent for an underaged monarch was the next person in line to the throne—in Victoria's case, King William's younger brother, the duke of Cumberland. But Cumberland was an evil man suspected of having committed murder, and no one wanted him to influence the heir to the throne.

The duchess used Cumberland's unpopularity to press her case. Finally Parliament passed legislation declaring the duchess to be Victoria's sole regent. However, the government did not award the duchess a title, nor did it give her any money of her own or of Victoria's.

Two days later, on September 8, 1831, the duchess refused to allow her daughter to attend King William's coronation. She used the excuse that Victoria's health was poor, but most people did not believe her. Newspaper reports suggested that the duchess wanted to punish the king because she had not gotten the money she wanted. Others speculated that she was angry over the order of the coronation procession, during which Victoria would not follow directly after King William but would be farther back in the line, behind his younger brothers.

Whatever her reasons, the duchess succeeded in keeping her daughter away from the event. Victoria was devastated. She wrote later that even her beloved dolls could not console her. Despite their presence she continued to weep "copious tears."[33] She resented her mother for keeping her apart from the king. The duchess said King William didn't really love her, but Victoria disagreed.

Though she was only twelve years old, the princess already understood her important position. She also knew her mother wanted to control the throne. She blamed John Conroy for this. Others blamed Conroy as well.

Queen Adelaide once tried to warn the duchess about Conroy's influence. She told her sister-in-law what the family had noticed:

> You are cutting yourself off more and more from them. This they attribute to Conroy, whether rightly or wrongly I cannot judge; they believe that he tries to remove everything which might obstruct his influence, so that he may exercise his power *alone*, and alone, too, one day reap the fruits of his influence. He cannot be blamed for cherishing dreams of future greatness . . . but everyone recognises these aspirations, towards which his every action is directed. [34]

Tours of the Countryside

Despite such warnings, the duchess remained loyal to Conroy. After she was declared regent she took his advice more than ever. She kept Victoria away from court and agreed with Conroy's suggestion that Victoria go on a series of tours throughout the countryside so her future subjects could get a good look at her. These tours were not quiet travels through pastoral settings. Instead they were grand, staged events with local honor guards, elaborate decorations, and lengthy speeches.

"Our carriage is drawn by grey horses," Victoria wrote on one of her tours, "the post boys have pink silk jackets, with black hats, and the horses have pink silk reins with bunches of artificial flowers." [35]

Victoria recorded these details in a journal given to her by her mother. She wrote in it every day, and by the end of her life she had filled more than one hundred volumes. However, only edited versions of her journals exist today. When Victoria died, she instructed that they be recopied to leave out anything sensitive; once the copies were complete, the originals were burned.

Still, the images she saw on her tours remain clear. Of a coal mining district she wrote:

When Victoria turned twelve, her mother began forcing her to go on a series of elaborately staged tours of the countryside so that the residents could see their future ruler.

The men, women, children, country and houses are all black . . . the grass is quite blasted and black. . . . The country continues black . . . everywhere, smoking and burning coal heaps, intermingled with wretched huts and carts and little ragged children.[36]

She also composed word pictures from which she would later make watercolor sketches. In one journal entry she notes: "Six fishermen in rough blue jackets, red caps and coarse white aprons, preceded by a band, bore a basket ornamented with flowers, full of fish as a present for us."[37]

John Conroy made all of the arrangements for Victoria's tours. The British press gave Conroy the name "Conroyal" because he acted as though he were a member of the royal family, giving orders and expecting them to be carried out. Primarily, Conroy wanted Victoria to act like a queen, even though she had not yet assumed the throne. Victoria knew this was an insult to King William. Later, she told Lord Melbourne that Conroy had forced her to

go [on] that tour about the country receiving addresses, which she, Victoria, very much disliked, and did all she could to prevent. She said "I knew it was improper, and very disagreeable . . . but it was all Sir John's influence, and what could I do?" [Conroy] made her mother do all the things she ought not.[38]

Victoria's tours infuriated King William. He hated what he called her "royal progresses," especially because most

The Little Amazon

In this quote from Monica Charlot's Victoria: The Young Queen, Caroline Bauer, a popular actress involved in a scandalous relationship with Victoria's Uncle Leopold, writes about the first time she and her mother met Victoria and the duchess of Kent.

"A clear girlish voice and a child-like laugh came ringing to our ears. On a silver-grey pony, accompanied by a large, white, long-haired dog, a young girl of eleven years came trotting up, fresh and round like a red rosebud with flying curls and large luminous eyes. These eyes looked at me so astonished and with such a gaze of inquisitive questioning in them, while the little hand securely held in the pony. And then all at once the little Amazon curved round, and presently returned with a stately round lady. She too started, and her eye glided all over us not without scrutiny, and I felt how I grew red with shame under this glance. Then the lady called to her little daughter a word in English, and both disappeared in the shrubbery leaving us behind in a deep sense of shame."

of her traveling companions were members of the Whig political party. The king and his followers belonged to the opposition Tory party, and they couldn't stand seeing a group of Whigs parading around the countryside as if they were in power.

"The King has been (not unnaturally) disgusted at the Duchess of Kent's progresses with her daughter through the kingdom,"[39] wrote the diarist Charles Greville. King William told his advisors he would find a way to stop these tours. He said they were bad for the country and bad for Victoria, making her "the object of party jealousy."[40]

But though King William ordered the duchess to stay at home, she kept traveling. "On what grounds can I be prevented making these visits?" she wrote to the prime minister. "I have for years done the same thing . . . with the happiest results to the Princess."[41]

More Arguments

At the same time, Conroy and the duchess were trying to keep Victoria away from anyone who might turn her against them. They specifically wanted to remove the girl's governess, Louise Lehzen, as well as Victoria's constant companion, the duchess of Northumberland, who had been hired to teach the princess proper court etiquette. Neither woman agreed with Conroy's opinions about how Victoria should be reared.

Conroy proposed a way to eliminate Lehzen and Northumberland. He drafted a letter to King William for the duchess to sign, saying that Victoria was too old for governesses or teachers. Instead, the letter explained, she now required only a lady-of-the-bedchamber, someone to help her with her personal needs. For this position the duchess suggested her own lady-in-waiting, Lady Flora Hastings.

Lady Flora was John Conroy's close friend. She went along with his ambitions. She hated Lehzen and treated her with such "contempt and incredible harshness" that the duchess of Northumberland wrote of it to Victoria's sister, Princess Feodora. Feodora replied:

> Dear Duchess [of Northumberland] we must do everything to preserve Baroness L[ehzen]. . . . The King is the person to uphold [Lehzen] and say she *must* and *shall* remain with the Princess . . . for what sort of person may be put near her, to further the plans of that man [Conroy].[42]

Feodora did not trust Lady Flora, who, according to Victoria, was "an amazing spy who would repeat everything she heard."[43]

King William was furious to hear of how badly Lehzen and the duchess of Northumberland had been treated. He not only refused to remove them from Victoria's household, but insisted that Northumberland handle all the arrangements for Victoria's confirmation, a religious ceremony scheduled to be held on July 30, 1835. He knew this would anger the duchess, and it did.

Thus the confirmation became yet another source of dispute. The duchess wanted the ceremony done her way, while the king wanted it his. In the end, Victoria's confirmation was not only performed according to King William's wishes, but when John Conroy arrived at the chapel, the king had him thrown out. The outraged duchess responded by refusing to allow Victoria to participate in any of the royal festivities that followed. She reminded her daughter that "until you are at the age of either 18 or 21 years . . . you are still confided to the guidance of your affectionate mother and friend."[44]

Another Tour

The following month, just to anger the king, the duchess planned another tour. This time Victoria did not want to go. She had just received a letter from King William asking her to remain at Kensington Palace. "I hope the newspapers will not inform me of your travelling this year," he wrote. "I cannot and therefore do not approve of your flying about the Kingdom as you have done the last three years."[45]

Victoria decided to stand up to her mother. The night before they were to leave, she told the duchess that under no circumstances would she go on any more tours. The two had a tremendous fight. Afterwards the duchess wrote Victoria a long letter. "You may imagine that I feel very much disappointed and grieved, that the journey we are to commence tomorrow is not only disagreeable to you, but that it makes you even unhappy." She added that if anyone else had heard their conversation, the princess "would fall in the estimation of the people of this country."[46]

Wracked with guilt, Victoria relented. She went on the tour as planned, but while traveling she complained of headaches, backaches, and fatigue. Conroy thought she was lying. Lehzen insisted that Princess Victoria was truly ill, but the duchess sided with Conroy and refused to call the doctor.

The duchess of Kent (pictured) did her best to keep Victoria away from anyone who might interfere with her plans to seize Victoria's future power.

By the end of the tour Victoria's condition had worsened. Still, she kept to her schedule. She left for a holiday on the coast, near Ramsgate Harbour, where she planned to meet with her Uncle Leopold. Leopold had become king of the Belgians in 1831 and was vacationing in England just so he could visit Victoria.

During their meeting, Leopold spoke to Victoria about her future as queen. Victoria noted in her journal:

He gave me very valuable and important advice. We talked over many important and serious matters. I look up to him as a Father, with complete confidence, love and affection. He is the best and kindest adviser I have. He has always treated me as his child and I love him most dearly for it.[47]

Leopold and Victoria had corresponded regularly over the years, and he knew of her difficulties with John Conroy. In fact, he sent his personal advisor, Baron Stockmar, to Kensington Palace to help Victoria in her dealings with Conroy. Stockmar found the man "vain, ambitious, most sensitive and most hot tempered," and he reported to King Leopold that Conroy's plan was to become Victoria's private secretary, a "dangerous" position that would give him access to royal documents and therefore a great deal of power.[48]

Conroy's Last Stand

After Leopold advised Victoria, he left England. She waved to his ship from the docks and afterwards collapsed from her illness. She had a high fever, and her mother finally decided to call the doctor. Victoria was confined to bed for five weeks, and Lehzen stayed with her day and night. The princess wrote in her journal:

> *Dear good* Lehzen takes such care of me, and is so unceasing in her attentions to me that I shall never be able to repay her sufficiently for it but by my love and gratitude. I never can sufficiently repay her for all she has *borne* and done for me. She is the *most affectionate, devoted, attached* and *disinterested* friend I have, and I love her most *dearly.* . . . I feel that I gain strength every day.[49]

But not everyone was as kind as Lehzen. While Victoria was at her weakest, John Conroy went to her room and in-

sisted she sign a paper declaring him her private secretary. "I resisted in spite of my illness and their harshness," Victoria later wrote, "my beloved Lehzen supporting me alone."[50]

Even after the princess recovered, Conroy kept badgering her. She was now seventeen years old, and the regency was due to end the following year. Unless Victoria became queen soon, Conroy would lose his chance to control the throne. His only other source of political power would be through the position of secretary. If he couldn't have that, then perhaps he could think of a way to extend the regency.

He began to speak openly of how inexperienced Victoria was. He told many

As Victoria, shown here at age sixteen, came closer to inheriting the crown, she had to fight off John Conroy's ambitious attempts to control the throne.

people in government that when Victoria reached eighteen she would still be too young to rule England. He suggested that the regency be extended to age twenty-one. After all, he argued, a child was still legally a minor until then. Stockmar reported Conroy's contention to King Leopold, adding, "God knows what schemes are being built on this fact."[51]

King William was also well aware of how dangerous Conroy had become. "I have great distrust of the persons by whom [Victoria] is surrounded,"[52] he told friends. At his seventy-first birthday celebration, the king rose to announce to the assembled guests—including Victoria and her mother—that he prayed that his

> life might be spared for nine months longer [when Victoria would turn eighteen], after which period, in the event of my death, no regency would take place. I should then have the satisfaction of leaving the Royal authority to the personal exercise of that Young Lady, the Heiress Presumptive of the Crown, and not in the hands of a person [the duchess] now near me, who is surrounded by evil advisers and who is herself incompetent to act with propriety in the station in which She would be placed.[53]

As Victoria's birthday approached, the king's health deteriorated. He decided it would be best to get her away from Conroy and the duchess as soon as the regency ended. He wrote her a letter offering her a special birthday present: a yearly income so that she could establish her own household apart from her mother's.

Conroy and the duchess were outraged. They made the weeping princess sign a letter they had written to the king refusing his offer. When he received the letter, King William insisted Victoria had not written it. But the duchess told her friends that her daughter had "of her own free will, told the King that she desires nothing but to be left as heretofore with her Mother."[54]

Still, the duchess knew her power over her daughter was ending. She was so upset at Victoria's eighteenth birthday celebration on May 24, 1837, that she didn't even stay for dinner. Later the duchess wrote a letter to the princess saying, "You are still very young, and all your success so far has been due to your *Mother's* reputation. Do not be *too sanguine* in *your* own *talents* and *understanding*."[55]

A Plot Against Victoria

Meanwhile, John Conroy remained defiant. During the birthday party, while others were dancing and celebrating in a grand ballroom, Conroy was brooding and plotting. Lehzen complained to the duchess of Northumberland that Conroy had been watching her the whole evening. The two women began whispering together, trying to figure out what Conroy would do now that Victoria was eighteen.

Conroy's plan was to convince everyone that Victoria was mentally unstable. He said she was flighty, childish, and more interested in clothing than in government. He told Lord Liverpool, a powerful Tory, that there was no way the girl could possibly assume the duties of a monarch—unless, of course, she had a competent private secretary. Conroy still hoped for this position, because it would enable him to control every aspect of Victoria's life.

The King's Anger

Furious that Victoria's mother was keeping her away from him, King William scolded both duchess and princess. His words, as quoted by biographer Cecil Woodham-Smith in Queen Victoria, *left Victoria in tears.*

"I have no hesitation in saying that I have been insulted—grossly and continually insulted—by that person [the duchess], but I am determined to endure no longer a course of behaviour so disrespectful to me. . . . I have particularly to complain of the manner in which [the princess] has been kept away from my Court . . . but I am fully resolved that this shall not happen again. I would have her know that I am King, and that I am determined to make my authority respected, and for the future I shall insist and command that the Princess do upon all occasions appear at my Court, as it is her duty to do."

Lord Liverpool went to see Victoria. She told him of her difficulties with Conroy and convinced Liverpool that she would be a capable ruler without Conroy's help.

But Liverpool could not end Conroy's scheming. No one could. He kept demanding that Victoria make him her private secretary. According to Stockmar, the princess continued to refuse, but "whether she will hold out, Heaven only knows, for [Conroy and the duchess] plague her, every hour and every day." Still, Victoria was "not at all inclined to do anything" to give Conroy any power. She was "deeply wounded" by the man's "impudent and insulting conduct," and "her affection and esteem for her mother seem likewise to have suffered."[56]

Then King William fell ill. As reports circulated that the king was dying, Conroy became more desperate. He told the duchess in front of witnesses, "if Princess Victoria will not listen to reason, *she must be coerced.*"[57] He wanted Victoria locked up somewhere until she agreed to sign a paper declaring him her private secretary.

But the duchess was afraid to go this far. Instead she yelled at her daughter, berating her to do what would empower her mother. "The struggle between the Mama and daughter is still going on," Stockmar reported. "[The duchess] is pressed by Conroy to . . . force her Daughter to do her will by unkindness and severity."[58]

Then, suddenly, it was too late. On June 20, 1837, King William died, and Victoria was queen.

From that moment on, Queen Victoria refused to have anything to do with her mother. "Poor woman," wrote Lord Holland, referring to the duchess. "The importance of her actions and opinions are gone."[59] And of John Conroy, Victoria rhymed: "Conroy goes not to Court, the reason's plain; /King John has played his part and ceased to reign."[60] She dismissed him from her household and began to rule England as an independent woman.

Chapter

3 Advisors and Enemies

Victoria was only eighteen years old when she assumed the throne, but she knew her own mind. On her first day as queen, she met with Great Britain's prime minister, Lord Melbourne, to tell him that she would keep him on as head of her affairs. Later she wrote that she had seen him "of COURSE *quite* ALONE as I shall *always* do all my Ministers."[61]

Lord Melbourne made a good impression on Victoria. In her journal on her first day as queen, she noted, "It had long been my intention to retain him . . . at the head of affairs and it could not be in better hands than his. . . . I like him very much and feel confidence in him. He is a very straightforward, honest, clever and good man."[62]

Conroy and the Duchess Try Again

Victoria's relationship with the prime minister upset her mother, who still insisted that Conroy should be advising the queen. The duchess wrote her daughter several letters pleading Conroy's case. In one she said, "You do not know the world. . . . [Conroy] has his faults, he may have made mistakes, but his intentions were always

Victoria accepts the news of her accession to the throne in 1837. Because she was eighteen years old, she was able to rule on her own without her interfering mother and the scheming John Conroy.

the best. . . . Take care that Lord Melbourne is not King."[63]

But Victoria was no longer listening to her mother. She had moved into separate apartments at Kensington Palace and ordered that the duchess could see her only by first sending a note asking permission. Victoria usually ignored these requests. She also made it clear that she wanted nothing whatsoever to do with Conroy.

Although Conroy realized that the power of the throne was no longer within reach, he could not give up so easily. He wrote to Lord Melbourne to demand compensation for all the things he had done for Victoria while she was growing up. He argued that he had sacrificed his career in the military to care for the princess and her mother and, therefore, deserved something in return. He was ready to retire to the country, he said, but first he wanted, among other things, a title, money, and a red ribbon honoring his service.

When Melbourne read Conroy's letter, he cried, "This is really too bad! Have you ever heard such impudence?"[64] Still, the prime minister wanted Conroy to leave London, so he decided to offer him a yearly pension. Conroy took the money, but refused to leave Kensington Palace.

"I never see [Conroy]," wrote Victoria to her Uncle Leopold, "nor does he meddle with my affairs but he still continues to tease me by ways and underhand means."[65]

The duchess continued to send letters to her daughter. Victoria wrote in her journal:

Spoke for some time of Ma [with Melbourne] . . . how much better it would

Royal Advice

After assuming the throne, Victoria continued to take advice from her uncle Leopold I, as these quotes from Giles St. Aubyn's book, Queen Victoria, *clearly show. The first is from one of Leopold's letters to Victoria, the second from the writings of diarist Charles Greville, clerk of the Privy Council.*

"'Whenever a question is of some importance,' wrote Leopold, 'it should not be decided on the day when it is submitted to you. Whenever it is not an urgent one, I make it a rule not to let any question be forced upon my *immediate* decision.'. . .

Two months later, Greville noted, 'When applications are made to Her Majesty, she seldom or never gives an immediate answer, but says she will consider it, and it is supposed that she does this because she consults Melbourne about everything, and waits to have her answers suggested by him. He says, however, that such is her habit even with him, and that when he talks to her upon any subject upon which an opinion is expected from her, she tells him she will think it over, and let him know her sentiments the next day.'"

Composed and confident, Victoria sits at the head of her first Privy Council, held at Kensington Palace in 1837.

be if Ma was not in the house and if she would go and visit her family; Lord Melbourne observed that that would be a great thing; for if she were to go away without going to her own family, it would be awkward and we should have to state the cause to the public; and make a cause of it.[66]

Three weeks after she assumed the throne, Victoria moved out of Kensington Palace altogether. She went to live at Buckingham Palace, away from her mother at last.

Victoria Performs Well

By this time, Victoria was a self-assured young queen. She had already attended her first Privy Council, a meeting of important government officials, where she had behaved more regally than anyone could have imagined. Charles Greville, who was the clerk of the Privy Council, wrote:

There never was anything like the first impression she produced, or the chorus of praise and admiration which is raised about her manner and behavior, and certainly not without justice. It was very extraordinary, and something far beyond what was looked for. Her extreme youth and inexperience, and the ignorance of the world concerning her, naturally excited intense curiousity. . . . [Lord Melbourne] asked if She would enter the room accompanied by the Great Officers of State, but She said She would come in alone. . . . She bowed to the Lords, took her seat, and then read her speech in a clear, distinct and audible voice, and without any appearance of fear or embarrassment. . . . She went through the whole ceremony (occasionally looking at Melbourne for instruction when She had any doubt what to do, which hardly ever occurred) and with perfect calmness and self-possession, but at the same time with a graceful modesty and propriety particularly interesting and ingratiating.[67]

Another witness to the meeting was a Tory who had not expected to like Queen Victoria because she favored the Whigs. Even he praised her behavior, writing:

I cannot describe to you with what a mixture of self-possession and feminine delicacy she read the paper. Her voice, which is naturally beautiful, was clear and untroubled; and her eye was bright and calm, neither bold nor downcast, but firm and soft. There was a blush on her cheek . . . and certainly she *did* look as interesting and handsome as any young lady I ever saw.[68]

"She not merely filled her chair," concluded the duke of Wellington, "she filled the room."[69]

At Buckingham Palace she became completely comfortable with her new role. "Everybody says that I am quite another person since I came to the throne," she wrote. "I look and am so very well, I have such a pleasant life; just the sort of life I like. I have a good deal of business to do, and all that does me a world of good."[70]

As clerk of the Privy Council, Greville also noticed how happy the queen was.

Everything is new and delightful to her. She is surrounded with the most exciting and interesting enjoyments; her occupations, her pleasures, her business, her Court, all present an unceasing round of gratifications. With all her prudence and discretion She has great animal spirits, and enters into the magnificent novelties of her position with the zest and curiousity of a child.[71]

A Joyful Time

And so the first months of her reign passed with great pleasure. She entertained friends, played chess, and went horseback riding, sometimes covering many miles in one day, and accompanied by as many as thirty other riders. She also enjoyed the company of dogs and children, and she allowed her young guests to play ball in the corridors of Buckingham Palace. All in all, the first summer of her reign was, as she wrote in her journal, "the pleasantest summer I EVER passed in *my life*."[72]

The following May the queen turned nineteen, and her official coronation was scheduled for June 28. In the weeks leading up to the event, Victoria attended numerous balls, parties, and concerts held in her honor. Meanwhile, the city of London was preparing for her crowning. Scaffolding was built so people could sit and watch the queen pass on her way from Buckingham Palace to Westminster Abbey, where the ceremony would take place. Crowds arrived by carriage, train, and ship, from all parts of the country and the world. They would hear bands, see fireworks, attend fairs, drink large quantities of gin and beer, and generally have a rousing good time. As Greville later said:

> There never was anything seen like the state of this town; it is as if the population had been on a sudden quintupled; the uproar, the confusion, the crowd, the noise, are indescribable. Horsemen, footmen, carriages squeezed, jammed, intermingled, the pavement blocked up with timbers, hammering and knocking, and falling fragments stunning the ears and threatening the head; not a mob here and there, but

the town all mob, thronging, bustling, gaping, and gazing at everything, at anything, or at nothing; the park one vast encampment, with banners floating on the tops of tents, and still the roads are covered, the railroads loaded with arriving multitudes.[73]

And he added, "The great merit of this Coronation is, that so much has been done for the people: to amuse and interest *them* seems to have been the principal object."[74] This was very different from previous reigns, when Britain's rulers didn't care what their subjects thought of them.

A Lavish Coronation

Lord Melbourne had always believed that public opinion mattered, and it was he who convinced Parliament to spend lavish sums on Victoria's coronation. In earlier times, a new queen could have ordered

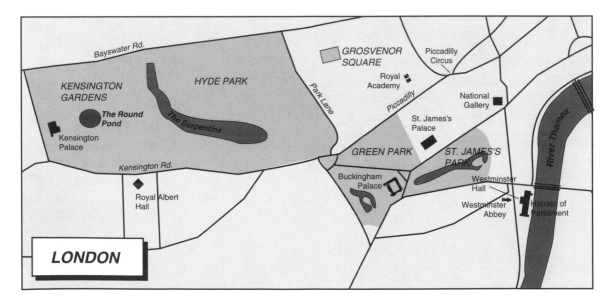

A crowned and bejeweled Queen Victoria poses regally in her coronation robes.

these expenditures herself. But by 1838 British law had begun to limit the power of the monarchy, and the queen's finances, like most other major issues, were controlled by the government. Parliament had to approve the expenditures to make the coronation magnificent.

On the day of the event, Victoria rode through the London sunshine in a beautiful carriage called the "State Coach." She wore fur-trimmed robes of crimson velvet that were edged with gold lace and tied with a golden cord. She had eight train bearers, each of them dressed in white and silver adorned with roses. At Westminster Abbey, she found breathtaking decorations in gold and crimson and saw over ten thousand spectators seated in the pews. Many of them wore jewels that caught the light coming through the windows and reflected it back against the walls as sparkling rainbows. When at last the archbishop of Canterbury crowned

her queen of England, she heard the sound of silver trumpets and the cheers of her subjects. She also saw her mother, who sat amidst the spectators, burst into tears.

Happiness Destroyed

Within a few months, the duchess of Kent was again causing her daughter trouble. She had followed Victoria to Buckingham Palace, moving in with her because she said it was considered improper for an unmarried woman to live without a lady of her own rank as a companion. Along with the duchess came John Conroy, whom the queen still hated.

The palace was filled with tension. Lord Melbourne complained about the duchess, calling her weak-minded, cold, and rude. The queen's ladies complained about the duchess's attendants, saying they were difficult and haughty. And Victoria complained about Conroy, telling Melbourne he had to find a way to get rid of the man.

Amid all of this turmoil, the joy ebbed from Victoria's life. She stopped getting up early and began to be careless about the way she dressed and groomed herself. She gained weight but refused to go on the walks Melbourne suggested. She was distressed about her prime minister's visits with a friend, Lady Holland, asking him whether he found that lady prettier than his queen. Lord Melbourne said he did not, but still Victoria was unhappy. Later she told Melbourne that she was unfit to be queen.

The Lady Flora Affair

She also complained of boredom, and indeed her evenings at the palace were filled with tedium. Her fights with her mother increased, and she frequently burst into tears. It was during this time that the event known as the "Lady Flora affair" occurred.

Lady Flora was still the duchess of Kent's lady-in-waiting, as she had been during the days when Conroy was trying to remove Governess Lehzen. Victoria had never trusted the woman, and now her distrust was worse than ever. When Lady Flora returned to the palace after a short absence, the queen watched her carefully.

Victoria immediately noticed that her mother's lady-in-waiting had gained weight. Then she discovered that Lady Flora was seeing a doctor, Sir James Clark, who was also her own physician. Victoria knew that this unmarried woman had

been spending a great deal of time alone with John Conroy. She jumped to one conclusion: Lady Flora was pregnant.

In 1839, an unmarried pregnant woman was scandalous. The household was soon in an uproar. The queen wrote in her journal:

> We have no doubt that she is—to use plain words—*with child!* Clark cannot deny the suspicion; the horrid cause of all this is the Monster and demon Incarnate, whose name I forbear to mention, but which is the 1st word of the 2nd line of this page [John Conroy].[75]

Faced with rumors, Sir James Clark, who had in fact treated Lady Flora only for sickness of the stomach and a pain in her left side, decided that she might possibly be pregnant. He asked her permission to do a more thorough examination. Lady Flora refused. She firmly denied that she was pregnant.

When Queen Victoria heard that Lady Flora would not allow Sir James to examine her, she ordered that the woman not appear in court again until she could prove she was innocent. Consequently Lady Flora relented and asked another physician, Sir Charles Clarke, to examine her. He said she was telling the truth about her condition.

An Outraged Public

Although the queen apologized, the incident soon took on grand proportions. Lady Flora wrote her family about the way she had been slandered, and her uncle had the letter published in a prominent newspaper. The public reacted with outrage. Soon other letters and editorials appeared, all of them opposed to the queen, her ladies, and Lord Melbourne.

Victoria reacted by treating Lady Flora worse than ever. She suggested that the woman's physician might have been mistaken. When Lady Flora took to her bed, Victoria scoffed. She refused to believe that Lady Flora was truly ill, even after Lord Melbourne himself insisted it was so. She also ignored the tears of her mother, who came to tell her that Lady Flora was dying.

It was several months before Victoria decided to judge Lady Flora's condition for herself. She went to visit the woman, and what she saw surprised her. As she later wrote in her journal:

> I went in alone; I found poor Lady Flora stretched on a couch looking as thin as anybody can be who is still alive; literally a skeleton, but the body *very* much swollen like a person who is with child; a searching look in her eyes, a look rather like a person who is dying; her voice like usual and a good deal of strength in her hands; she was friendly, said she was very comfortable, and how very grateful for all I had done for her, and that she was glad to see me looking well. I said to her, I hoped to see her again when she was better upon which she grasped my hand as if to say "I shall not see you again." I then instantly went upstairs and returned to Lord Melbourne who said "You remained a very short time."[76]

A week later, Lady Flora was dead. The public reacted with more outrage. They hissed and booed Victoria whenever she went out riding and shouted coarse insults at her at public events. Some even called her "Mrs. Melbourne."

Newspapers again published articles and pamphlets against the queen. Editorials accused Victoria of being more concerned with parties, dances, and concerts than with people. Many suggested that she needed to appoint new advisors, new ladies-in-waiting, and particularly a new royal physician.

John Conroy had already left. Some months earlier, perhaps sensing what was to come, he abruptly left England for Italy, where he remained for years. When he returned to Britain, it was to retire in the town of Reading, away from London and the political turmoil of the royal court.

Lady Flora (pictured) was the unfortunate victim of rumors started by Victoria. The incident led to a sharp decline in Victoria's popularity.

Slandered and Persecuted

Newspapers and pamphlets criticized the queen for slandering Lady Flora. In her book Victoria: The Young Queen, *Monica Charlot includes excerpts from two pamphlets, the first entitled* The Dangers of Evil Counsel *and the second* The Palace Martyr!

". . . the cause here advocated is that of female innocence, slandered and persecuted to death: it is the cause of the weaker party, oppressed by power; it is the cause of British justice and liberty; it is the cause of the character and honour of the Queen's court; it is the cause of our innocent young Queen herself 'surprised,' 'betrayed' by evil suggestions and evil counsel into that which she knew not."

"Strange destiny that Britain's mighty isle
Should hang dependent on a school girl's smile;
The court physician, with his cringing back
And coward sneer, the leader of the pack;
While titled beldames their assistance brought,
And the young Queen smiled blithely on the sport."

The British media and the public severely criticized Victoria (pictured) for slandering Lady Flora.

A Change of Government

Victoria was too distracted to enjoy Conroy's departure. Her government was undergoing tremendous change.

Within one branch of Parliament, the House of Commons, the majority party had long been the Whigs, also known as the Liberals. The Whig Party represented political reform. It was founded in the late 1600s by people who helped force King James II from his throne after he became a Roman Catholic. Its members, mostly middle-class landowners and industrialists, were responsible for many of the laws that limited the power of the British monarch.

In contrast, the Tory Party supported King James. Its members, called Conservatives, believed that all kings had a divine right to rule no matter what their beliefs or behavior. Most Tories were country gentry, a social class that fell just below nobility, or they came from merchant classes or official administerial groups. They opposed change and favored isolationism, which meant that they did not believe England should become involved in foreign affairs.

As the minority party, the Tories had little power. The prime minister was customarily a member of the majority party, and it was he who appointed and supervised most of the important positions within the government. The prime minister also ran the Cabinet meetings and advised the queen, who had the right to dissolve Parliament at any time in favor of a general election. In this position Lord Melbourne, therefore, had a great deal of influence over which laws were passed in the House of Commons. If a vote was not coming out the way he wanted it to, he could threaten to ask Queen Victoria to end Parliament.

But because of the Lady Flora affair, Lord Melbourne had become very unpopular with the public, and the Tories used his unpopularity to deepen people's opposition to the Whig Party as a whole. Voters began replacing Whigs with Tories in the House of Commons. Soon the Tory Party was the majority.

Lord Melbourne had no choice but to resign in favor of a Tory prime minister. He knew this would upset the queen, who hated Tories and loved Melbourne. He implored her to "meet this crisis with that firmness which belongs to your character and with that rectitude and sincerity which will carry your Majesty through all difficulties."[77]

Still, Victoria was in tears. She did not want the Tories to control her government,

Victoria's sketch of Lord Melbourne. Much to the queen's dismay, Melbourne, who had always acted as her trusted advisor, was forced to resign when the Tory Party gained power.

"How Low, How Sad I Feel"

This excerpt from Victoria's diary as quoted in Lytton Strachey's book Queen Victoria, *shows how upset she was that her prime minister, Lord Melbourne, would have to leave office if his party, the Whigs, lost power to the Tories.*

"I cannot say (though I feel *confident* of *our success*) HOW *low*, HOW *sad* I feel, when I think of the POSSIBILITY of this excellent and truly kind man not *remaining* my Minister! Yet I trust fervently that *He* who has so wonderfully protected me through such manifold difficulties will not *now* desert me! I should have liked to have expressed to Lord M. my anxiety, but the tears were nearer than words throughout the time I saw him, and I felt I should have choked, had I attempted to say anything."

The prospect of ruling without her trusted prime minister, Lord Melbourne, deeply saddened the young queen.

and she could not believe that her beloved Melbourne would no longer be advising her. She instantly disliked his replacement, Sir Robert Peel, and made her opinion quite clear. At their first meeting, she treated him coldly. Her coldness turned to anger when he told her she would have to give up her Whig ladies-in-waiting in favor of Tory women. Later she wrote to Lord Melbourne:

> Sir Robert Peel has behaved very ill, and has insisted on my giving up my Ladies, to which I replied that I would never consent, and I never saw a man so frightened. . . . I was calm but very decided, and I think you would have been pleased to see my composure and great firmness; the Queen of England will not submit to such trickery. [78]

But although Peel appeared frightened, he need not have worried. Victoria was very different from King George IV, who had not only openly insulted his prime minister, the earl of Liverpool, but covertly plotted against him. She was also very different from King George III, who had threatened members of Parliament so they wouldn't vote for a plan he opposed. Unlike her predecessors, Queen Victoria was not prone to violent action. Instead she used quiet stubbornness to get her own way.

Her argument with Peel continued for four days. He insisted that she could not have as her ladies-of-the-bedchamber a group of women who were the wives of his political opponents. She insisted that she was the queen and could include whomever she wanted in her innermost circle. Finally, Peel realized he could not work with Victoria. He resigned, and the next day Melbourne returned as prime minister, even though he was a Whig.

Regaining the Public's Favor

The public admired the queen for standing up for her rights in a calm yet firm manner. They praised her strong character and now shouted "Bravo" when she went out riding. She had proved herself to be an exemplary monarch.

Nevertheless, she had many political enemies. The Tories, furious that their prime minister had been forced to resign, began to criticize the monarchy. Many of the queen's supporters, including Lord Melbourne, felt that the only way to strengthen Victoria's rule was to find her a husband. Marriage and children would be a sign of the security and stability of both the queen and the succession. And so, even though to her "the whole subject was an odious one, and one which I hated to decide about," [79] Queen Victoria prepared to meet with the most likely candidate: her cousin, Prince Albert of Coburg.

4 A Royal Marriage

Victoria had first met Albert in 1836, during the festivities surrounding her seventeenth birthday. Even then, he was being considered as her future husband.

Albert was just three months younger than Victoria. His father, the duke of Coburg, was brother to the duchess of Kent, and his uncle was the same as Victoria's, King Leopold of the Belgians.

Leopold had been promoting the match for years, as had the rest of the Coburg family. From the time he was a little boy, Prince Albert knew he was expected to marry Princess Victoria. To this end he was schooled in all the social graces and intellectual skills necessary for the husband of the queen of England.

First Impressions

When at last Albert was ready to meet Victoria, he was extremely nervous. His nerves, combined with all the late-night festivities of Victoria's birthday, took their toll on him. "Poor, dear Albert," Victoria noted in her journal, ". . . looked very pale and felt very poorly." Later, after dancing, he "turned pale as ashes; and we all feared he might faint."[80]

Still, she had a good impression of him. In her journal she remarked on his handsomeness, kindness, and intelligence. Discussing all the cousins who had been brought to meet her—Prince Albert, his brother Ernest, and Princes Ferdinand and Augustus, who were the sons of another Coburg uncle—she remarked:

> Dearly as I love Ferdinand, and also good Augustus, I love Ernest and Albert *more* than them, oh yes, MUCH *more*. . . . They have both learnt a good deal, and are very clever, naturally clever, particularly Albert, who is the most reflecting of the two, and they like very much talking about serious and instructive things and yet are so *very very* merry and gay and happy, like young people ought to be; Albert always used to have some fun and some clever witty answer at breakfast and everywhere.[81]

But when Victoria became queen and with Lord Melbourne as prime minister, all thoughts of Albert were temporarily set aside. Melbourne did not like the idea of Victoria marrying a foreign prince. Still, he couldn't envision her marrying one of her subjects. And then there was the problem of her mother. As Victoria noted in her journal:

Said to [Lord Melbourne] how dreadful it was to have the prospect of torment for many years by Mama's living here, and he said it was dreadful, but what could be done? She had declared (some time ago) I said she would never leave me as long as I was unmarried. "Well then, there's *that* way of settling it," he said. That was a schocking [sic] alternative, I said.[82]

But when her Uncle Leopold arranged for her to receive a second visit from Albert and his brother Ernest in October 1839, Victoria found that her sentiments towards marriage had changed. "It was with some emotion that I beheld Albert— who is beautiful,"[83] she wrote.

Four days later the prince noted that he had been told "that V. had almost decided to choose me as her future husband and would probably make her declaration personally to me [soon]."[84] This she did on the following day, October 15, and the wedding was set for February 10. In the meantime, Prince Albert would return to Coburg to prepare for his permanent move to England.

His departure was marked by tears and kisses. "I cried much," Victoria wrote in her journal that night, "wretched, yet happy to think that we should meet again so soon! Oh! how I love him, how intensely, how devotedly, how ardently!"[85]

Albert soon wrote to her of his affections.

I need not tell you that since we left all my thoughts have been with you at Windsor and your image fills my whole soul. Even in my dreams I never imagined that I should find so much love on earth. How that moment shines for

Victoria's sketch of Albert. Victoria took an immediate liking to the young prince and chose him as her husband.

me when I was close to you, with your hand in mine. Those days flew by so quickly, but our separation will fly equally so.[86]

The Prince's Role

While Prince Albert was gone, the queen officially announced her betrothal. Immediately the British government began debating her future husband's title. Victoria wanted Albert named "King Consort," so he could rule by her side. But many members of Parliament, particularly the Tories, opposed giving the foreign-born prince so much power.

Victoria's uncles, who were still next in line for the throne, were particularly outspoken against making Prince Albert any kind of king. They feared he might claim the throne for himself if the queen died childless.

Others opposed the title for a different reason. They believed it would weaken the British monarchy. They felt that if Parliament were allowed to create a king, then one day it might try to take the crown away from someone it decided was undeserving. "If you once get the English people in the way of making kings," Lord Shaftesbury said, "you will get them into the way of unmaking them."[87] This would mean that birthright would no longer matter. As a result, many people feared that calling Albert the king of England was the first step towards changing the country from a monarchy into a democracy.

After much discussion, Parliament made Prince Albert a British subject but gave him no title, no rank in the army, no English peerage (which would have given him a seat in the House of Lords as a member of Parliament), and no right to succession before any children he and Victoria might have. In short, it gave him no power whatsoever. In addition, Parliament granted him a smaller monetary allowance than was customary for the spouse of a monarch.

Queen Victoria was furious. She never forgave her uncles for their opposition to her wishes, and she railed against the Tories who controlled Parliament. "Monsters!" she called them in her journal.

Victoria Engaged

In a journal entry dated 15 October 1839 and quoted in Christopher Hibbert's Queen Victoria in Her Letters and Journals, *Victoria writes of the moment she asked Albert to marry her.*

"At about 1/2 p. 12 I sent for Albert; he came to the Closet where I was alone, and after a few minutes I said to him, that I thought he must be aware why I wished [him] to come here, and that it would make me too happy if he would consent to what I wished (to marry me); we embraced each other over and over again, and he was so kind, so affectionate; Oh! to feel I was, and am, loved by such an Angel as Albert was too great delight to describe! he is perfection; perfection in every way—in beauty—in everything! I told him I was quite unworthy of him and kissed his dear hand—he said he would be very happy [to marry me] and was so kind and seemed so happy, that I really felt it was the happiest brightest moment in my life, which made up for all I had suffered and endured. Oh! how I adore and love him, I cannot say!! how I will strive to make him feel as little as possible the great sacrifice he has made; I told him it was a great sacrifice,—which he wouldn't allow . . . I feel the happiest of human beings."

Then she added, "You Tories shall be punished. Revenge, revenge!"[88] But she did not plot against them or resort to violence, as previous monarchs might have done. Instead she simply refused Albert's request that his household staff include an equal number of both Tories and Whigs.

"It Will Not Do"

"The Whigs are the only safe and loyal people,"[89] she had told him a few weeks earlier. Now her renewed hatred for the Tories made her even more resolute. She wrote to him in Coburg:

> As to your wish about your gentlemen, my dear Albert, I must tell you quite honestly that it will not do. You may entirely rely upon me that the people who will be round you will be absolutely pleasant people of high standing and good character . . . you may rely upon my care that you shall have proper people and not idle and not too young and Lord Melbourne has already mentioned several to me who would be very suitable.[90]

Albert was upset that the queen was going to choose his servants and advisors for him. Once he and Victoria married, they would maintain separate households; in other words, within the same residence they would each have their own set of attendants. Albert didn't understand why his bride-to-be wouldn't allow him to manage his own household. He already had several people in mind for key positions. He replied to Victoria's letter:

> Think of my position, dear Victoria; I am leaving my home with all its old associations, all my bosom friends, and going to a country in which everything is new and strange to me—men, language, customs, modes of life, position. Except yourself I have no one to confide in. And is it not even to be conceded to me that the two or three persons who are to have the charge of my private affairs should be persons who already command my confidence?[91]

But the queen would not give in to her future husband. She wrote back:

> Though I am very anxious you should not appear to belong to a Party, still it is necessary that your Household should not form a too strong contrast to mine, else they will say, "Oh, we know the Prince says he belongs to no party, but we are sure he is a Tory!" Therefore it is also necessary that it should appear that you went with me in having some of your people who are staunch Whigs.[92]

Faced with Victoria's stubbornness, Albert realized he would never change her mind. He told the queen he would accept anyone she appointed to serve him.

On other matters, too, he was no match for her. When he requested a lengthy honeymoon, Victoria replied:

> You forget, my dearest love, that I am the Sovereign, and that business can stop and wait for nothing. Parliament is sitting, and something occurs almost every day, for which I may be required, and it is quite impossible for me to be absent from London; therefore two or three days is already a long time to be absent. I am never easy a moment, if I am not on the spot, and see and hear

what is going on, and everybody . . . says I must come out after the second day, as I must be surrounded by my Court. This is also my own wish in every way. [93]

Albert soon realized that no one except Lord Melbourne could change Victoria's mind on anything. As the wedding day approached, he showed signs of despair. He still longed for the honor of a British title and felt he had been mistreated. He didn't understand that it would be illegal for the queen to grant him a lordship on her own. "It needs but the stroke of your pen to make me a peer and to give me an English name," [94] he wrote to her.

Victoria tried to explain the situation to him.

The English are very jealous of any foreigner interfering in the government of this country and have already in some of the papers expressed hope that you would not interfere. Now, though I know you never would, still, if you were a Peer, they would all say, the Prince meant to play a political part. [95]

Albert interpreted this to mean that Victoria herself did not want him to have a role in the British government. This added to his discouragement. "My future lot is high and brilliant," he wrote to a friend, "but also plentifully strewn with thorns." [96]

Wedding Day

But on February 6, 1840, Albert put his doubts aside and sailed across the English Channel to meet his bride. The crossing was rough. "I never remember having suf-

Victoria poses in her wedding gown before her marriage to Albert in 1840.

fered so long or so violently," he wrote to the queen upon landing. "Our reception was satisfactory. Thousands were standing on the quay, and greeted us with loud and continuous cheering." [97] An honor guard escorted him to London, and on February 8, two days before the wedding, he met with Victoria at Buckingham Palace.

She had been awaiting his arrival under a cloud of misery. She was so nervous about the upcoming ceremony that she had fallen ill. She had also been fighting furiously with her mother, who wanted to continue living in the palace after the wedding. But after Albert visited with her, Victoria felt calm. "Seeing his *dear dear* face again put me at rest about everything,"[98] she wrote.

She awoke just before 9 A.M. on the rainy morning of February 10, 1840, eager to become his bride. Breaking tradition, she rushed to see him before the wedding, but first she sent him a note.

> How are you today and have you slept well? I have rested very well, and feel very comfortable today. What weather! I believe however the rain will cease. Send one word when you, my most dearly loved bridegroom, will be ready. Thy ever-faithful 'Victoria R.'[99]

Despite the queen's wishes, the weather did not improve. In fact, it grew worse, with more rain and terrible winds, but this did not discourage a large crowd from watching the royal procession pass through the streets from Buckingham Palace to the Chapel Royal in St. James's Palace, where the ceremony would be held. It was the first time in over a century that a royal marriage had taken place in public during the day; always before they had been private, nighttime affairs.

The chapel itself was crowded with people. They watched as Albert took his place at the altar, before which were two stools to be used by the bride and groom during the ceremony. Prince Albert was

A crowd looks on as Victoria and Albert join hands during their simple but well-attended wedding ceremony.

wearing the uniform of a British field marshal, and he had entered to the music of "See the Conquering Hero Come."

The queen walked down the aisle to the music of the national anthem. She was wearing a white satin dress decorated with orange blossoms, and a wreath made of the same flowers sat on her head. Her twelve young bridesmaids were dressed in simple white tulle gowns and carried white roses.

The ceremony too was simple, but there were a few awkward moments. The bridesmaids had difficulty carrying the train of the queen's dress, and later they giggled when they should have been quiet. Albert was unsure what to do, not having rehearsed, and sometimes he stumbled over his words. Also, Victoria's mother, according to a newspaper report in the *Times*, "appeared somewhat discon-

King Leopold Praises Albert

In this letter excerpt from Monica Charlot's Victoria: The Young Queen, *King Leopold explains why Prince Albert would make a good husband for Victoria.*

"If I am not very much mistaken he possesses all the qualities required to fit him completely for the position he will occupy in England. His understanding is sound, his apprehension clear and rapid, and his feelings in all matters appertaining to personal appearance are quite right. He has got powers of observation and possesses much prudence, without anything about him that could be called cold or morose."

King Leopold thought Albert (pictured) possessed all the suitable qualities to become Victoria's husband.

solate and distressed, and we fancied, but it might be fancy, that we saw the traces of tears upon her countenance."[100]

The ceremony was followed by the wedding breakfast, a meal that the new couple shared with close friends and family at Buckingham Palace. It included an elaborate wedding cake that was more than nine feet around and sixteen inches high. Important people who had not been invited to the breakfast had their own cakes delivered to them as a consolation—a total of one hundred had been baked, in a variety of sizes and styles.

A Preference for Simplicity

When the breakfast was over, the young couple changed to traveling clothes and left for Windsor Castle. As Greville noted:

> They went off in a very poor and shabby style. Instead of the new chariot in which most married people are accustomed to dash along, they were in one of the old travelling coaches, the postillions in undressed liveries, and with a small escort, three other coaches with post horses following.[101]

Queen Victoria was proving to be very different from previous monarchs, who had showed a marked preference for extravagance. She found great happiness in simplicity.

She also found great happiness in Albert, and in this too she was unusual. Previous monarchs had chosen their mates with dispassionate calculation. Political alliances were important. Faithfulness, on the other hand, was not. Even Victoria's uncle, King William IV, had fathered ten illegitimate children. Royal infidelity was extremely common, and the British people had come to view their rulers as an immoral lot.

But with Victoria and Albert, the public saw something special. They eagerly showed their approval of the marriage as the couple rode by in their carriage. Victoria wrote in her journal:

> There was an immense crowd of people outside the Palace, and which I must say never ceased until we reached Windsor Castle. Our reception was most enthusiastic and hearty and gratifying in every way; the people quite deafening us; and horsemen and gigs etc. driving along with us. We came through Eton where all the Boys received us most kindly—and cheered and shouted. Really I was quite touched.[102]

Still, by the time she reached Windsor, Victoria had a terrible headache. Though she managed to eat dinner with Albert, she was then forced to lie on a sofa for the rest of the evening.

> My *dearest dearest* Albert sat on a footstool by my side, and his excessive love and affection gave me feelings of heavenly love and happiness I never could have *hoped* to have felt before! He clasped me in his arms, and we kissed each other again and again! His beauty, his sweetness and gentleness—really how can I ever be thankful enough to have such a *Husband!* —. . . to be called by names of tenderness, I have never yet heard used to me before—was bliss beyond belief! Oh! this was the happiest day of my life!—May God help me to do my duty as I ought and be worthy of such blessings![103]

Husband and Wife

Although it was true that Victoria was deeply in love with her new husband, she was also queen of England, and as she had explained to Albert some time earlier, she would not shut herself away for a conventional honeymoon. The day after the wedding she hosted a dinner party for ten. The day after that she held another, larger party. On her third day of marriage, she returned to London and her royal duties, with an unhappy Albert trailing along.

Three months later the prince wrote to a friend that he was "the husband, not the master of the house."[104] Victoria did not allow him to interfere in any way with the management of her household, giving those duties instead to her former governess, Baroness Lehzen. Albert resented his exclusion, and he complained about Lehzen to his advisor, Baron Stockmar. Stockmar had once served the couple's uncle, King Leopold. Now he wrote to Leopold about the matter. Leopold in turn wrote to Victoria with this advice:

> The Prince ought in business as in everything to be necessary to the Queen . . . he should be to her a walking dictionary for reference on any point which her own knowledge or education have not enabled her to answer. There should be no concealment from him on any subject.[105]

Prince Albert and Queen Victoria at the time of their marriage. After they had been married a short while, Albert became unhappy that Victoria would not allow him a more active part in political decision making.

Melbourne's Influence

Lord Melbourne was not necessarily a good influence on Victoria, as biographer Woodham-Smith explains in Queen Victoria.

"One of the very few valid criticisms of Queen Victoria is that she was not sufficiently concerned with improvement of the conditions in which a great mass of her subjects passed their lives. She lived through an age of profound social change, but neither public health, nor housing, nor the education of her people, nor their representation, engaged much of her attention. . . . Some part of what was lacking . . . must be attributed to the influence of Melbourne. At an impressionable period, made doubly impressionable by the deprivations of her earlier life, it was unfortunate that she should have come under the influence of a man with so much charm and so little belief in human nature, with such a touching capacity for tenderness allied to dislike of reform, and such want of sympathy with the struggling mass of the workers that he was capable of callousness."

But to King Leopold's dismay, although Prince Albert always took his advice, Queen Victoria did not. She continued to ignore her husband's views on anything of any importance and refused to discuss politics with him at all.

Finally Lord Melbourne spoke to her on Albert's behalf. The queen remained uninfluenced. "My impression is that the chief obstacle in Her Majesty's mind is the fear of difference of opinion," Lord Melbourne said after the discussion, "and she thinks that domestic harmony is more likely to follow from avoiding subjects likely to create difference."[106]

Trouble was brewing. Albert was clearly upset, and there were rumors that he did not love Victoria. Then something happened to change the couple's relationship: the queen became pregnant. As the months passed, she withdrew from many of her duties, and Albert took them over. Victoria allowed the prince's influence to expand. For once she was more preoccupied with her own condition than with British politics.

5 Head of the Household

Queen Victoria had not wanted to become pregnant so soon after her wedding and expressed her displeasure:

> I must say that I could not be more unhappy. I am really upset about it and it is spoiling my happiness; I have always hated the idea and I prayed God night and day to be left free for at least six months, but my prayers have not been answered and I am really most unhappy. I cannot understand how any one can wish for such a thing, especially at the beginning of a marriage.[107]

She had been Albert's wife for only two months when she discovered she was expecting.

A few weeks later, Victoria's health was threatened—not from her condition but from an assassin. A man with a pistol fired upon the queen while she was out riding in her open carriage. He missed, then fired again. Albert pulled Victoria down, and a crowd of onlookers grabbed the would-be assassin.

Although the man was later sent to an insane asylum, many people, including Prince Albert and Frau Lehzen, believed that he was completely sane. There was some evidence that he might have had a connection to the king of Hanover, Ernest Augustus, because the gunman possessed letters postmarked from Hanover and his gun supposedly bore the initials E.R., for Ernestus Rex (King).

King Ernest was Victoria's uncle, the younger brother of William IV and formerly the duke of Cumberland, the same man whom people feared would kill Victoria when she was a baby. Now that Victoria was queen of England, King Ernest often said she had no right to wear the crown. Citing the Salic Law of Succession, an ancient principle followed by most European countries that decreed only males could inherit the throne, he argued that Britain should not allow any woman to be its reigning monarch. Nevertheless, no one could prove that Ernest had any involvement in the assassination attempt.

Admired Again

Many other such incidents occurred throughout Victoria's reign, but in each case, the would-be assassin was judged to be insane rather than part of a conspiracy. Meanwhile, the queen bore these threats against her life with outward calm. She refused to end her public appearances. People appreciated her courage, and after the first assassination attempt,

Assassination Attempts

Queen Victoria experienced several assassination attempts during her reign. She wrote about one of them in this letter to her Uncle Leopold, dated May 31, 1842.

"On returning from the chapel on Sunday, Albert . . . suddenly turned to me and said it appeared to him as though a man had held out a pistol to the carriage. . . . No one, however, who was with us . . . had seen anything at all. Albert began to doubt what he believed he had seen. Well, yesterday morning (Monday) a lad came . . . and said that he saw a man in the crowd as we came home from church, present a pistol to the carriage, which, however, did not go off, and heard the man say, 'Fool that I was not to fire!' The man then vanished. . . . The boy accordingly was sent to Sir Robert Peel, and (doubtful as it all still was) every precaution was taken, still keeping the thing completely secret . . . we drove out—many police then in plain clothes being distributed in and about the parks, and the two Equerries riding so close on each side that they must have been hit, if anybody had. . . . All was so quiet that we almost thought of nothing,—when, as we drove down Constitution Hill, very fast, we heard the report of a pistol, but not at all loud, so that had we not been on the alert we should hardly have taken notice of it. We saw the man seized by a policeman next to whom he was standing when he fired, but we did not stop. . . . The boy identified him this morning."

they forgot the Lady Flora affair and began to wave and cheer Victoria whenever she went outside.

They also stopped criticizing Prince Albert. Everyone admired him for protecting Victoria's life. Newspapers praised him for remaining cool under pressure. This recognition of the prince's strengths led Parliament to appoint him regent, which meant that he would be in charge of his son or daughter should Victoria die during childbirth. It was a position of power, and Albert was thrilled.

Children Bring Changes

On November 21, 1840, Victoria's baby was born. It was a girl—the Princess Royal, Victoria Adelaide Mary Louisa, called "Vicky" for short—and when the queen heard she had given birth to a princess, she replied, "Never mind—the next time it will be a Prince."[108]

Less than a year later, she did indeed have a son. The Prince of Wales was born on November 9, 1841, and named Albert Edward; his parents immediately nicknamed him "Bertie."

Albert doted on both children. He was upset when Baroness Lehzen took complete charge of the nursery. He felt she was "a crazy, common, stupid intriguer, obsessed with lust of power, who regards herself as a demi-god,"[109] and he didn't want her to raise his son and daughter. When he came home from a trip to find Vicky looking pale and thin, he exploded with

With the birth of the royal couple's first child, Vicky, Albert began to take on more of the responsibilities of the throne.

rage. He told the queen that Lehzen had to go, and the two of them had a huge fight. Victoria ran off in tears, but for once Albert would not give in. "There can be no improvement till Victoria sees Lehzen as she is,"[110] Albert told Baron Stockmar. Later he added, "Victoria is too hasty and passionate for me to be able often to speak of my difficulties. She will not hear me out but flies into a rage and overwhelms me with reproaches of suspiciousness, want of trust, ambition, envy, etc. etc."[111]

Faced with Albert's newfound assertiveness, Queen Victoria backed down. Lehzen was retired to Germany, and the royal couple's relationship was permanently altered. Albert began offering advice more and more, and the queen found herself disagreeing with him less and less. Later Victoria would write:

> So many girls think that to marry is *merely* to be independent and amuse oneself—whereas it is the very *reverse* of independence—2 wills have to be *made* to act together and it is *only* by *mutual* agreement and *mutual yielding* to one another that a happy marriage can be arrived at.[112]

Many in the royal court noticed that Victoria was now adopting Albert's views. Albert's secretary, George Anson, said that the prince was reeducating the queen and "reforming her mind."[113] Others noted that Victoria no longer enjoyed London or its parties, preferring instead the quiet life of the country, like her husband. She went along with his decision to buy an estate in Osbourne, on the Isle of Wight, where the family could spend time walking along the seashore or through the woods. She also gave him free reign to reorganize her household and cut costs.

Albert and Victoria attend the theater with their children Bertie and Vicky.

By giving her husband so much power, Victoria was different from previous female monarchs. Queen Elizabeth I had avoided marriage altogether, and Queen Mary I and Queen Anne had turned to their ministers rather than to their mates for advice. Queen Mary II did share decisions with her husband, King William III, but that was because he had been crowned alongside her as a co-sovereign.

Most Britons approved of Victoria's behavior. They viewed her role in the royal marriage as proper and believed she was maintaining a good balance between

Victoria on Becoming a Mother

In this letter excerpt from Monica Charlot's biography Victoria: The Young Queen, *Victoria writes to her eldest daughter about the experience of pregnancy.*

". . . aches—and sufferings and miseries and plagues—which you must struggle against—and enjoyments etc. to give up—constant precautions to take, you will feel the yoke of a married woman. . . . I own it tried me sorely; one feels so pinned down—one's wings clipped—in fact, at the best (and few were or are better than I was) only half oneself—particularly the first and second time. This I call the shadow side. . . . And therefore I think our sex a most unenviable one."

her responsibility to her husband and her duty to her country. Moreover, they considered their queen to be a symbol of all that was best about their society. This positive public opinion was very important to the monarchy system. It lessened the risk that a revolution might occur and open the door for democracy.

Queen Victoria strengthened the monarchy even more by providing the throne with a long succession of heirs. On April 25, 1843, she gave birth to Princess Alice Maud Mary, followed by Prince Alfred Ernest Albert (nicknamed "Affie") on August 6, 1844. Princess Helena Augusta Victoria was born two years later, then Princess Louise Caroline Alberta two years after that. Prince Arthur William Patrick Albert was born in 1850, Prince Leopold George Duncan Albert in 1853, and Victoria's last child, Princess Beatrice Mary Victoria Feodora (nicknamed "Baby"), in 1857.

Victoria loved her nine children dearly. Her family was lively and fun loving, and Albert remained a doting father. He spent a great deal of time with his children, playing hide-and-seek or giving them piggyback rides. "He is so kind to them," Victoria wrote, "and romps with them so delightfully, and manages them so beautifully and firmly."[114]

Family Life

Each royal child had a unique personality. Vicky was smart but difficult, while her sister Alice was amiable and loved music. Bertie, who stammered, was slow-witted and prone to tantrums. Helena was a tomboy who sometimes punched her brothers. Louise was a beautiful girl who loved to paint and draw. Beatrice, called "Baby," was very spoiled. Alfred, known as "Affie," was cheerful, industrious, and reckless. He was always taking risks and getting scolded; he was also his father's favorite son. Victoria's favorite son was Arthur, who was fascinated with all things military and told everyone he wanted to be a soldier.

In contrast, Arthur's younger brother, Leopold, had no such hopes. He was a sickly child who bruised easily; the doctors soon discovered that he had hemophilia. Victoria worried about him constantly and tried to keep him from hurting himself.

Hemophilia is an incurable disease that causes severe bleeding with every injury. Its symptoms occur only in males; a female carries the disease in her genes without suffering from it.

Victoria was the first member of the royal family to be identified as a carrier of hemophilia. (Later, Vicky, Alice, and Beatrice would also be identified as carriers.)

Victoria was not afraid to embrace new techniques in medicine. She was also the first to use chloroform to ease her pains during childbirth. Years earlier, as a girl, she was the first royal to be vaccinated against childhood disease.

Victoria worried a great deal about Bertie, who would be king someday. He was failing at his studies, and his tantrums continued. Victoria feared he would be unfit to rule. What would happen then?

The queen had no concerns over Vicky's future. When the girl was ten, she met Prince Frederick William of Prussia, and began exchanging letters with "Fritz." Soon it was clear that the two would marry someday. Victoria was pleased when the match was arranged, although

Victoria and Her Children

After a trip away from them, Victoria wrote about her children in this journal entry dated November 3, 1844, as quoted in Elizabeth Longford's biography Victoria R.I.

"The children again with us, & such a pleasure & interest! Bertie & Alice are the greatest friends & always playing together.—Later we both read to each other. When I read, I sit on a sofa, in the middle of the room, with a small table before it, on which stand a lamp & candlestick, Albert sitting in a low armchair, on the opposite side of the table with another small table in front of him on which he usually stands his book. Oh! if I could only exactly describe our dear happy life together!"

An 1846 painting of the royal family. From left to right: Alfred, Bertie, Victoria, Albert, Alice, Helena, and Vicky.

she despaired at the thought of her oldest daughter living so far away.

Victoria was preoccupied with her children throughout their lives. She spoke of them constantly, missed them when she traveled, and took them with her as much as possible. She and Albert often let the oldest ones skip their lessons in favor of a trip to the zoo, circus, or theater.

However, the queen was not completely indulgent. She and Prince Albert insisted that the boys learn to farm, build, and do other chores, while the girls were taught cooking, sewing, and similar tasks. The children also attended certain social events where they were expected to behave properly. If they did not behave well, either in public or at home, they received a whipping.

Prince Albert was the ultimate disciplinarian in the family. He made sure his children followed the rules, which were, he said, "difficult to uphold in the face of so many women" running the nursery. He always gave "the final judgement," saying, "From my verdict there is no appeal. Unfortunately, also I am the executive power and have to carry out the sentence."[115] Albert had high morals and was unyielding in his beliefs.

A New Advisor

By the time Lord Melbourne finally resigned as prime minister in August 1841, the queen was relying completely on Albert for all her decisions. As Melbourne himself noted, "It is so different now from what it would have been [had my resignation been final] in 1839—the Prince un-

Bertie's failure in his studies and his frequent tantrums caused Victoria to worry that her son might not be fit to rule.

derstands everything so well, and has a clever, able head."[116]

Though Victoria had always met with Lord Melbourne privately, she conferred with his successor, Prime Minister Robert Peel, in Albert's presence. The prince suggested public policy and proposed new laws, including one that made dueling illegal, and the queen decided he could meet with people on her behalf. Even when Albert was not in the room, Victoria often replaced the pronoun *I* with *we* in her sentences, as though she were two people instead of just one. Prince Albert shared not only her throne but her innermost thoughts. He remained by her side as she faced a series of new political crises both at home and abroad.

Chapter

6 Political Decisions

The transition from Melbourne to Peel as prime minister in 1841 meant that the Tories were fully in control of the British government. In earlier days, Victoria had been upset when the Whigs lost power. Now she was more accepting. She ushered in the new Tory ministers with such grace and calm that the diarist Greville noted:

> This struck me as a great effort of self-control, and remarkable in so young a woman. Taking leave is always a melancholy ceremony, and [those] whom she thinks are attached to her, together with all the reminiscences and reflections which the occasion was calculated to excite, might well have elicited uncontrollable emotions. [117]

She also allowed three of her Whig ladies-of-the-bedchamber to be replaced, though not without shedding some tears.

Over the next few years, Victoria came to admire Prime Minister Peel. She called him "a man of unbounded *loyalty, courage,* patriotism, and *high-mindedness,* and his conduct towards me has been *chivalrous* almost, I might say." [118] Part of the queen's admiration might have stemmed from Peel's close association with her husband. Albert and Peel often discussed politics. By 1845, Greville noted, Albert and Victoria were "one person, and as he likes and

Victoria admired Prime Minister Robert Peel, calling him "a man of unbounded loyalty."

she dislikes business, it is obvious that while she has the title, he is really discharging the functions of the Sovereign. He is King to all intents and purposes." [119]

But Victoria's absence from the political arena would not last much longer. In July 1846, soon after the birth of the

Victoria Criticized

According to diarist Greville, as quoted in Cecil Woodham-Smith's biography, Queen Victoria, *the British public was outraged when the queen, who supposedly loved animals, attended a slaughter of corralled deer.*

"Nothing can exceed the universal indignation felt here by people of every description at the brutal and stupid massacre of the deer which Albert perpetrated and at which she assisted. It has been severely commented on in several of the papers, and met by a very clumsy (and false) attempt to persuade people that She was shocked and annoyed. No such thing appeared and nothing compelled her to see it. But the truth is, her sensibilities are not acute, and though she is not at all ill-natured, perhaps the reverse, she is hard-hearted, selfish and self-willed."

queen's third child, Robert Peel resigned. Having failed to receive enough support for one of his reform laws, the prime minister followed custom and yielded his office to the opposing party. The Whigs were in control again. The new prime minister was Lord John Russell, who chose Lord Henry Palmerston as his foreign secretary.

The queen thought both men incompetent. Lord Russell irritated her by seeking other people's opinions after asking for hers, while Lord Palmerston's political opinions were completely contrary to her own. Palmerston favored constitutional governments rather than complete monarchies. He was outspoken in his beliefs, and there was a history of antagonism between Lord Palmerston and Prince Albert. Consequently, Queen Victoria felt he should be replaced as foreign secretary.

Her relationship with Palmerston worsened after the man made a terrible blunder. In a message to the French ambassador, he suggested that Prince Leopold of Coburg, Germany, who was the son of Victoria's Uncle Ferdinand, would make a good husband for Queen Isabella of Spain. When the king of France heard this, he became furious.

Earlier, Queen Victoria had promised the French king Louis Philippe that England would never propose such a match. Victoria had felt that she could make this promise because, although recent laws had reduced her influence in Parliament, she still made decisions on foreign affairs that related to personal (as opposed to military) matters. Palmerston's remark had placed her in a very bad position.

The king of France accused Victoria of breaking her word and said he was no longer obliged to support an agreement he had made with England in 1845. At that time, King Louis Philippe had pledged that there would be no marital alliance between his country and Spain.

Now he contacted the Spanish royal family and arranged two marriages. The first was between Queen Isabella and her Spanish cousin, who was unable to father children. The second was between Queen Isabella's sister and King Louis Philippe's own son. The match was unlikely to produce an heir to the Spanish throne. It would also permanently unite France and Spain.

Queen Victoria rebuked Lord Palmerston for causing this disaster. But because Palmerston saw the powers of the monarch as extremely limited, he didn't worry about the queen's opinion of him. Still, his wife warned him against being so bold.

> You fancy [Victoria] will hear reason, when in fact all you say only proves to her that you are determined to act on the line she disapproves, and which she still thinks is wrong. . . . You always think you can convince people by arguments, and she has no reflection or sense to feel the force of them. [120]

Lord Palmerston ignored his wife's advice. He continued to argue with Victoria, and because of his views on the monarchy, he repeatedly made decisions and acted on them without consulting her. On one occasion he sent his own version of a dispatch rather than Albert's. Victoria scolded him by letter:

> Lord Palmerston has a perfect right to state to the Queen his reasons for disagreeing with her views, and will always have found her ready to listen to his reasons; but she cannot allow a servant of the Crown and her Minister to act contrary to her orders, and this without her knowledge. [121]

Victoria's letter had no effect on Lord Palmerston, who continued to do and say whatever he pleased. He voiced his approval of revolutions, and in 1848, when uprisings occurred in Germany, Switzerland, Austria, Denmark, and Italy, he was slow to offer support to the leaders of those countries. Again both Queen Victoria and Prince Albert complained about Palmerston to Parliament. They wanted the foreign secretary replaced. Nevertheless, the man remained in office. A popular politician, he had many powerful supporters, and even Prime Minister Russell did not dare to dismiss him.

Albert Takes the Blame

In December 1851 Lord Palmerston made a more serious mistake. He spoke in favor of Napoleon III's recent overthrow of the French government, despite Parliament's decision that Britain should remain neutral on the issue. As a result, his popularity dipped. This time when Victoria called for Palmerston's dismissal, Prime Minister Russell agreed.

But Lord Palmerston was not so easily undone. Even though he was no longer foreign secretary, he was still a powerful man, and he used his considerable influence to end Russell's control of Parliament. Under a new prime minister, Palmerston was able to obtain another position in the Cabinet. Meanwhile he continued to disagree openly with the policies of the queen.

He was particularly outspoken when the Russians invaded the Turks' territory, and the Turks threatened to retaliate. The queen talked of peace, but Palmerston advocated war. Soon the trouble between Turkey and Russia grew worse. The Turks

When Britain failed to intervene between the battling Turks and Russians in 1851, the public and the press blamed Prince Albert, speculating that he had influenced Parliament's decision to remain neutral.

ken out, they logically say the interest of the Coburg family, which is Russian, Belgian etc., is preferred to the alliance with Louis Napoleon [of France]."[122]

Victoria suspected that Lord Palmerston was behind the attacks on Albert that appeared in the press. She was upset over the treatment of her husband. Then in January 1854, Parliament praised Prince Albert and declared their support for him. Victoria was thrilled and wrote:

> The position of my beloved lord and master has been defined for *once and all*, and his merits have been acknowledged on all sides most duly. There was an immense concourse of people assembled when we went to the House of Lords, and the people were very friendly.[123]

The Crimean War

declared war on Russia, and France decided to help the Turks fight.

Members of Parliament were faced with a dilemma. They wanted peace, but if Russia succeeded in overrunning the Turks, it might next decide to encroach on British territory. The government debated whether to join the battle. Victoria again expressed her desire for peace, but this was not her decision to make. Parliament had the power to declare war.

Still, when Britain failed to act, rumors spread that Albert was to blame. People speculated that the prince had somehow influenced Parliament. After all, he was a foreigner from a family that had ties to Russia. "The people have generally made me their scapegoat," the prince wrote to his brother. "Because war has not yet bro-

Two months later, Britain finally declared war on Russia and sent its military to join the French and Turkish soldiers in an invasion of the Crimean peninsula, which was Russian territory. The fighting was intense, and not only bullets but disease and winter's cold killed many men.

Queen Victoria followed the events of the Crimean War closely. It was easy for her to do this because the war was the first ever to be recorded by war reporters and photographers, and as she recorded the number of dead and the details of various battles in her journal each day, Victoria wished she were playing a larger role in the campaign. To her daughter Helena she wrote, "I regret exceedingly not to be a man and to be able to fight in the war.

My heart bleeds for the many fallen, but I consider that there is no finer death for a man than on the battlefield!"[124]

The queen regretted that she could not be involved in any of the military decisions of the war. That responsibility fell to her government and its commander in chief, a position held first by Lord Hardinge and then, when he resigned, by Victoria's cousin, George, duke of Cambridge. While these men and their generals directed the troops on the battlefield, Prince Albert sat at a palace desk and thought up various military improvements, which Britain's military leaders promptly rejected.

A frustrated Victoria decided to put her energy into supervising relief efforts for the wounded and organizing ladies' aide committees. She personally visited hospitals to cheer patients and invited convalescents to visit her at the palace. She knitted socks and mittens for the men at the front. She wrote condolence letters to war widows. She publicly praised the efforts of Florence Nightingale to improve sanitary conditions at British army hospitals overseas. She even told the War Office to send blankets to the military horses. In short, she did the best she could to ease the suffering of all those involved in the war.

Victoria followed the Crimean War (pictured) closely and wished she could become more involved in the military decision making, which was left to her government and the commander in chief.

Throughout the Crimean War, Victoria decorated its heroes with special medals. This was her duty as queen, but she also enjoyed the awards ceremonies a great deal. However, she did not agree with the custom of giving officers a different kind of medal than regular soldiers. She believed that a hero was a hero regardless of rank or social position. As a result, after the Crimean War finally ended in 1856, she created one single medal that could be awarded to *any* individual who had shown bravery in battle. Initially cast from the bronze of captured Russian guns, this medal was called the Victoria Cross, and it was very popular with the public. Victoria personally pinned the cross on each recipient's uniform during elaborate public ceremonies.

By this time, Lord Palmerston had been named prime minister, and Victoria's feelings about him had changed.

Albert & I agreed that of all of the Prime Ministers we have had, Lord Palmerston is the one who gives the least trouble, & is the most amenable to reason & most ready to adopt suggestions. The great danger was foreign affairs, but now that . . . he is responsible for the *whole*, everything is quite different.[125]

On Military Hospitals

In his biography Victoria, *Stanley Weintraub describes Victoria's reaction to the condition of certain military hospitals during the Crimean War.*

"'The buildings were bad,' she charged, 'the wards more like prisons than hospitals, with the windows so high that no one can look out of them,—and most of the wards are small, with hardly [any] space to walk between the beds. There is no dining-room or hall, so that the poor men must have their dinners in the same room in which they sleep, and in which some may be dying, and at any rate suffering, while others are at their meals.' She had heard of a proposal to utilize old, no-longer-seaworthy ships to house convalescents, an idea she sniped at by declaring such a hulk 'a very gloomy place, and these poor men require their spirits to be cheered as much as to have their physical sufferings attended to.' Such matters, she declared, were 'constantly in her thoughts, as indeed is everything connected with her beloved troops, who have fought so bravely, and borne so heroically all their sufferings and privations.'"

Princess Vicky stands with her bridegroom, Prince Frederick of Prussia, in a photo taken a few days after their 1858 wedding.

A Baby and a Wedding

Confident in Palmerston at last, Victoria could turn her attention to her private life. She needed all her energy to deal with the birth of her youngest child, Princess Beatrice, in April 1857, followed in January 1858 by the marriage of her eldest child, Princess Vicky. The queen found both events depressing. She disliked being pregnant and was unhappy with many of the details of Vicky's wedding. She felt Albert was not spending enough time with her and quarreled with him.

Although her depression lifted when her baby was born, Victoria continued to have difficulty balancing the responsibilities of being a wife and mother with those of being a monarch. She wanted to spend time with her children. However, she had to sign most official documents, meet with her ministers, preside over public ceremonies, attend diplomatic functions, and appear at formal events. In public and in private, she wanted Albert to remain by her side, and she complained whenever he left her alone.

But though the prince clearly loved his wife, he refused to be her devoted servant. He had his own interests to pursue. He told Victoria to worry less about herself and more about the outside world. England was undergoing many changes, and he urged her to pay attention to them.

7 Problems and Progress

The England of the late 1850s was no longer the country of Victoria's youth. For one thing, the population had more than doubled. With this increase came a host of problems, including overcrowding, poverty, malnourishment, and disease.

In addition, the structure of British society was changing. No longer was England controlled solely by wealthy, titled, rural landowners. Members of the urban middle class, and later the working class, gained a voice in government as Parliament passed a series of reform bills that expanded their right to hold public office and vote.

Although Queen Victoria did not propose these reforms, she did sanction some elevation of the middle class. After all, unlike previous monarchs, she had much in common with ordinary people. She was a wife and mother in a stable family with many children. She also enjoyed the same leisure activities as many of her subjects, attending such popular events as circuses and waxwork exhibits and reading the novels of Charles Dickens, a contemporary writer who often depicted the widespread poverty of Victoria's England.

She was very aware of what life was like for her less fortunate subjects. During her wartime hospital visits and committee meetings, she had spent a lot of time in the company of average Britons. She desired "a better feeling, and much greater union of classes"[126] and said that she "would as soon clasp the poorest widow in the land to my heart as I would a queen or any other in high position."[127]

Victoria realized that with or without her support, change was inevitable. To Princess Vicky she wrote, "The Lower Classes are becoming so well-informed—are so intelligent & earn their bread & riches so deservedly that they cannot & ought not to be kept back—to be abused by the wretched ignorant Highborn beings, who live only to kill time."[128] Still, she did not believe in revolution, nor did she believe that the monarchy should be abolished. She remained convinced that the traditional system was for the common good.

The Great Exhibition

Yet for all her sympathy for the poor as individuals, Queen Victoria did not work towards helping them as a group. She did not press for radical changes in the class structure of her people, nor did she campaign against their oppression. It was Prince Albert who took up the cause of

In 1851 Prince Albert planned the Great Exhibition as a way to expose the poor to modern technology. The exhibit was housed in a huge glass and iron structure dubbed the "Crystal Palace."

improving the living conditions of the poor.

The prince was active in a variety of charitable causes, but his most memorable achievement was the Great Exhibition of 1851. The prince conceived of the Great Exhibition as a way to help working-class families "soar to a nobler fuller life . . . on the strong wings of art and science."[129] He would expose them to everything that modern technology and creativity had to offer by creating a "world industrial exhibition" that would feature "the achievements of modern invention."[130]

Albert labored tirelessly to raise money for the exhibition. It required a huge building, and no existing one would do. The prince decided to have a huge iron and glass structure built in Hyde Park. Newspapers called it the "Crystal Palace."

Inside the eighteen-acre building, exhibits were arranged into four categories—raw materials, machinery, manufactures, and fine arts. There were 13,937 exhibitors, 7,381 from Great Britain and her colonies and 6,556 from forty different foreign countries.

Albert and the Great Exhibition

"I am more dead than alive from over-work. The opponents of the Exhibition work with might and main to throw all the old women into a panic, and to drive myself crazy. The strangers, they give out, are certain to commence a thorough Revolution here, to murder Victoria and myself, to proclaim the Red Republic in England. The plague is certain to ensure from the confluence of such vast multitudes, and to swallow up those whom the increased prices of everything has not already swept away. For all this I am to be responsible, and against all this I have to make efficient provision."

Everything displayed had to be the most modern of its type. Exhibits featured recent inventions like the locomotive, the textile machine, the printing machine, and the telegraph, along with new advances in decorating and home furnishings. People could also admire fine porcelain, tapestries, embroidery, and other fine arts. They could eat new foods like ice cream and jelly. These refreshments had previously been enjoyed only by the upper classes, but here their price, like the admission fee, was affordable.

The Great Exhibition was a huge success. From its opening on May 1, 1851, to its closing five months later, more than six million people came to see the exhibits and taste the food. The queen herself visited almost every day. "It was such a time of pleasure, of pride, of satisfaction & of deep thankfulness," she noted in her journal, "it is the triumph of peace & good will towards all,—of art, of commerce,—of my beloved Husband—& of triumph for my country."[131]

Troubles Ahead

But despite her joy, Victoria was worried. Albert had been working too hard; he looked tired, pale, and old, despite the fact that he was only in his thirties. He complained of stomach cramps and was often ill. Yet he refused to slow down.

Prince Albert was not the queen's only worry. Trouble was brewing in India, which was administered jointly by Great Britain and a private business, the East India Company. The East India Company maintained order with its own army. Its Indian soldiers, trained by Europeans, were known as *sepoys*.

In 1857 the sepoys in the region of Bengal rebelled. At the city of Meerut, near Delhi, they murdered or abused hundreds of Europeans, including women and children. Other sepoys in other cities soon joined the rebellion. The queen wrote to her Uncle Leopold, "We are in sad anxiety about India, which engrosses all our attention. Troops cannot be raised fast, or largely enough. And the horrors committed on the poor ladies—women and children—are unknown in these ages and make one's blood run cold."[132]

As she had been during the Crimean War, Victoria was powerless; she could only watch and wait. However, during this military campaign her prime minister was Lord Palmerston, and she was not afraid to offer him her opinions quite aggressively. She told him exactly what he should do, and surprisingly, he sometimes listened.

Finally the uprising was quelled and Parliament ordered the East India Company to transfer all control of India to the Crown of England. The queen found her new territory "a source of great satisfaction and pride" and called it "so bright a jewel of her Crown, and which she would wish to see happy, contented, and peaceful."[133] She promised that England would improve the welfare of the Indians and not interfere with native customs or religious beliefs.

Other countries now demanded the queen's attention as well. To protect India, British troops had been sent to Persia. There had also been fighting in Asia, to protect the British colony of Hong Kong from the Chinese. Regarding these and other matters, Queen Victoria continued

The 1857 rebellion in Bengal pitted the British against the sepoys. After the fighting subsided, England gained control of all of India.

to offer Lord Palmerston her opinions. She sent messages to Parliament on a variety of military and foreign policy concerns.

At the same time, she was facing problems at home. The first involved her daughter Vicky, who married and left England in January 1858. Queen Victoria missed her terribly. "Yes it is cruel, very cruel," she wrote, "very trying for parents to give up their beloved children, and to see them go away from the happy peaceful home."[134] She was even more upset when, only a few months later, Vicky became pregnant. The queen wrote of her unhappiness in a series of letters to her daughter in which she complained about pregnancy, childbirth, being a wife, and other personal matters.

Vicky's baby, Prince William, was born in January 1859. The delivery was difficult; Vicky almost died and the baby's left arm was permanently damaged. Victoria, at age thirty-nine, was excited about being a grandmother but also worried about the health of her daughter, especially when Vicky became pregnant again less than a year later.

Worrying About Bertie

The queen was also still worried about Bertie. Unlike his younger brother Affie, who was in training for the navy, Bertie was not a serious young man. The heir to the throne was more devoted to parties and clothes than to his studies, first at the University of Edinburgh and then at Oxford. Victoria did not think he was suited to be the next king of England.

She complained about him in her letters to Vicky. Bertie was "lively, quick and sharp when his mind is set on anything, which is seldom," the queen said of her son. "Usually his intellect is of no more use than a pistol packed at the bottom of a trunk if one were attacked in the robber-infested Apennines."[135]

When Victoria's eldest daughter, Princess Vicky (pictured), married and left England in 1858, Victoria missed her terribly.

Both Albert and Victoria were concerned about whether their son Bertie, shown during his visit to America in 1860, would be able to handle the challenges of inheriting the throne.

Though he could be charming, Bertie had extreme fits of rage that appeared with little warning. Both Victoria and Albert were concerned about how he would behave when he became king. They decided to test him. In 1860, just before his nineteenth birthday, they sent him on a tour of Canada and the United States. In Canada, he was scheduled to appear at a variety of public ceremonies. In the United States, he would travel incognito, as an ordinary student touring the countryside.

It was the first time an heir to the British throne had crossed the Atlantic Ocean. Cheering crowds greeted him in Canada. At all official events, he behaved extremely well. He was polite and did not lose his temper. In the United States, he showed an energy and enthusiasm that appealed to his hosts and he was a very popular guest.

The queen was pleased. She wrote Vicky that Bertie "really deserves the highest praise."[136] But Albert did not share these feelings. He still doubted his oldest son's abilities. He was also unhappy with

"An Ugly Baby Is a Very Nasty Object"

In this excerpt from Christopher Hibbert's Queen Victoria in Her Letters and Journals, *Victoria writes of her distaste for infants.*

"Abstractedly, I have no *tendre* for them [babies] till they have become a little human; an ugly baby is a very nasty object—and the prettiest is frightful when undressed—till about four months; in short as long as they have their big body and little limbs and that terrible frog-like action. But from four months, they become prettier and prettier."

Ostrich Eggs

As her lady-in-waiting, Marie Mallet, wrote in this letter to her family (excerpted in Victor Mallet's book, Life with Queen Victoria)*, sometimes the queen was remarkably naive.*

"The Queen paid a visit to a Zoo Garden near here belonging to a certain Comtesse de la Grange . . . and was presented with a new-laid ostrich egg; this was carefully blown by the chef and its contents manufactured into an omelette which Her Majesty pronounced delicious. On the egg the doubtful Comtesse had scrawled her name, 'Just as if she had laid it herself,' remarked the Queen quite naively! Then added, 'Why cannot we have ostrich eggs at Windsor? We *have* an ostrich.' 'Yes, mama, a male one,' was Princess Beatrice's amused reply."

American newspaper reports that said Bertie had been flirting with women during his trip.

Prince Albert decided it was time to find his son a wife. He proposed several suitable matches, but Bertie turned them all down. Albert renewed his efforts. He also sent Bertie back to school, admonishing him to become more studious than before.

Victoria watched this struggle between son and husband with concern. About Bertie she wrote, "I feel very sad about him, he is so idle and so weak. God grant that he may take things more to heart and be more serious for the future, and get more power. The heart is good, warm and affectionate."[137]

The queen was equally concerned about Albert's health. The stress of dealing with Bertie's future was proving too much for him. As the year 1861 began, he suffered from a variety of complaints, including toothaches, insomnia, and more stomach pains. He was also experiencing fevers and chills. But while the queen took note of her husband's illnesses, she did not realize just how sick he was.

8 The Shadow of Grief

Victoria wrote of Albert's poor health in letters to Vicky. Sometimes her words showed little sympathy. Of his toothache she said:

> I hope, however, it is a little better today, but dear Papa never allows he is any better or will try to get over it, but makes such a miserable face that people always think he's very ill. It is quite the contrary with me always; I can do anything before others and never show it, so people never believe I am ill or ever suffer. His nervous system is easily excited and irritated and he's so completely overpowered by everything.[138]

Once the doctors confirmed that Albert did indeed have a dental problem and would have to undergo gum surgery, Victoria was more compassionate.

> It has been a most trying, wearing and distressing time, for I could not bear to see him suffer so much and to be so despondent and weak and miserable— I would so willingly have borne it all for him; we women are born to suffer and bear it so much more easily, our nerves don't seem so racked, tortured as men's are![139]

Despite his poor health, Albert refused to decrease his workload. The

This photo appeared on Albert and Victoria's 1861 calling card. The same year, Albert's health began to fail rapidly.

queen grew frustrated. "My greatest of all anxieties is that dearest Papa works too hard," she wrote to Vicky, and "wears himself quite out by all he does."[140]

Death of the Duchess

But Albert's illnesses seemed mild in comparison to those of Victoria's mother. The duchess of Kent was now seventy-five years old and suffering from erysipelas, a serious disease that caused skin and tissue swelling.

Ever since John Conroy had left court, Victoria and her mother had found it easier to get along. They eventually developed a very close relationship, and once Victoria had children, the two women spent a great deal of time together. By all accounts, the duchess had become remarkably pleasant and agreeable. She doted on her grandchildren, and Victoria often asked her advice about raising them.

Therefore, when in March 1861 the duchess of Kent's medical condition suddenly worsened, Victoria was distraught. The queen wrote after visiting her mother:

Oh! what agony, what despair was this! . . . I knelt before her, kissed her dear hand and placed it next my cheek; but, though she opened her eyes, she did not, I think, know me. She brushed my hand off, and the dreadful reality was before me, that for the first time she did not know the child she had ever received with such tender

An Intimate Portrait

A member of the court, who witnessed the royal family's last Christmas together in December 1860, writes about how ordinary they seemed. This quote is taken from Stanley Weintraub's biography Victoria.

"I have never seen a much more agreeable sight. It was royalty putting aside its state and becoming in words, acts, and deeds one of ourselves—no forms and not a vestige of ceremony. Even as in a public bazaar, where people jostle one another, so lords, grooms, Queen, and princes laughed and talked, forgot how to bow, and freely turned their backs on one another. Little princesses, who on ordinary occasions dare hardly to look at a gentleman-in-waiting, in the happiest manner showed each person they could lay hands on the treasures they had received. . . . Prince Arthur (the flower of the flock) speedily got into a volunteer uniform, which, with endless other things, including a little rifle, fell to his lot, took a pot-shot at his papa, and then presented arms."

smiles! I went out to sob . . . I asked the doctors if there was no hope. They said, they feared, none whatever.[141]

Within hours the duchess was dead.

Victoria's grief was almost boundless. She sobbed and fell into a deep depression. "The dreaded terrible calamity has befallen us," she wrote, "which seems like an awful dream. . . . Oh God! how awful how mysterious! . . . the constant crying was a comfort and relief. . . . But oh! the agony of it!"[142] For the queen, death was a new experience. She confided to her journal that she had never been near a coffin before.

Victoria's mourning lasted for months. It was so excessive that Albert began to worry about her. He decided to take her on a trip to lift her spirits.

They journeyed to the Scottish Highlands in October 1861. They had a home there, called Balmoral, and the area was Victoria's favorite place. As she traveled, she grew more cheerful. On one excursion away from Balmoral, she and Albert covered more than 120 miles in two days on horseback. They had great fun, but when they got back to England, Victoria's depression returned.

More Bad News

Victoria's mental state was worsened by some more tragic news. In November, telegrams came from Portugal announcing that both Prince Ferdinand and King Pedro V had died of typhoid fever. Victoria and Albert were related to the Portuguese royal family, and Albert had been friends with King Pedro for years.

The prince was even more upset by the deaths than Victoria. He could not recover from the shock of what had happened. Then he received more distressing news: Bertie was in trouble.

Albert had allowed the twenty-year-old to leave his studies to attend a ten-week course in military training held in Dublin, Ireland. While there, Bertie had met a young actress named Nellie Clifden. He had brought her back to Windsor with him, and now the two were the subject of much gossip.

Prince Albert was enraged. He felt Bertie was jeopardizing the throne. The British public had criticized other monarchs for having affairs, and Albert did not want his son held up to future ridicule. Albert wrote Bertie an angry letter, in which he said that Bertie was no longer "an ornament to a great and powerful and religious nation" but someone "who has sunk into vice and debauchery."[143] He added that should Nellie become pregnant, she would claim that Bertie was the father. Prince Albert wrote to his son:

> If you were to try and deny it, she can drag you into a Court of Law to force you to own it & there with you in the witness box, she will be able to give before a greedy Multitude disgusting details of your profligacy for the sake of convincing the Jury, yourself cross-examined by a railing indecent attorney and hooted and yelled at by a Lawless Mob!! Oh horrible prospect, which this person has in her power, any day to realise! and to break your poor parents' hearts.[144]

Later Albert went to Bertie's school to talk with him in person. Bertie apologized for his behavior. He ended his relationship

"It Is *Too* Touching"

In a letter to her Uncle Leopold (quoted in Cecil Woodham-Smith's Queen Victoria), *Victoria describes her feelings as she looked through her deceased mother's possessions.*

"[I was struck by] how very very much she and my beloved Father *loved* each other. *Such* love and affection. I hardly knew it was *to that extent*. Then her love for *me*— It is *too* touching; I have found little books with the accounts of my babyhood, and they show *such* unbounded tenderness! Oh! . . . To miss a Mother's friendship, not to be able to have Her to confide in when a girl *most* needs it . . . drives me *wild* now."

with Nellie and asked that the intimate details of his affair be kept from the queen. Albert agreed.

"I Should Not Struggle for Life"

But although the incident was resolved, Albert never really recovered from it. His health worsened. He told Victoria, "I do not cling to life. I am sure, if I have a severe illness, I should give up at once, I should not struggle for life."[145]

By now the prince was unable to keep food down. He took to his bed, yet he was too restless to stay there. He kept changing rooms, sleeping at first in one place and then another. He developed fevers and chills and had trouble breathing. He was also occasionally delirious.

At first the doctors felt his illness was nothing serious. Then they suspected typhoid, even though he had not been exposed to it. It was also possible he had

cancer of the stomach or bowels. The doctors continued to encourage the queen.

She remained optimistic. In her journal she noted that Albert's illness would probably soon pass. She wrote to her Uncle Leopold, "I do not sit up with [Albert] at night, as I could be of no use; and there is nothing to cause alarm."[146] Daughter Alice, who had become Prince Albert's nurse, tried to tell the queen otherwise, but she would not listen. Victoria told Lord Palmerston her husband merely had "a feverish cold."[147]

Finally Alice herself let the other children know that their father was dying. She summoned them to the palace, where they gathered at his bedside. Prince Albert had recently moved into the room where both King George IV and King William IV had died. When the queen walked in, she saw that "the room had the sad look of night-watching, the candles burnt down to their sockets, the doctors looking anxious."[148]

Albert's appearance distressed her.

There was what they call a dusky hue about his face and hands, which I knew was not good. . . . Albert folded his arms, and began arranging his hair, just as he used to do when well and he was dressing. These were said to be bad signs. Strange! as though he were preparing for another and greater journey."[149]

The queen left for a while, then came back to sit beside her husband's bed. He spoke to her in German—"*Gutes Fräuchen,*" he said, meaning "good wife." Then he kissed her and fell asleep.

When Albert awoke he called for his family and the members of his household. They came to him one after another. It was December 14, 1861, and in her journal entry for that date, Victoria noted what happened when it was her turn to pay her last respects:

> I bent over him and said to him *"Es ist Kleines Fräuchen"* [it is your little wife] and he bowed his head; I asked him if he would give me *"ein Kuss"* [a kiss] and he did so. He seemed half dozing, quite quiet . . . I left the room for a moment and sat down on the floor in utter despair. Attempts at consolation from others only made me worse . . . Alice told me to come in . . . and I took his dear left hand which was already cold, though the breathing was quite gentle, and I knelt down by him. . . . Two or three long but perfectly gentle breaths were drawn, the hand clasping mine and . . . all, all, was over. I stood up, kissed his dear heavenly forehead and called out in a bitter and agonising cry, "Oh, my dear Darling!"[150]

Prince Albert was dead, and Queen Victoria was plunged into despair. All of England worried about her. "What will happen," said one member of the royal household, "where can She look for that support and assistance upon which She has leaned in the greatest and least questions of her life?"[151] In other words, what was Victoria without Albert?

"Heartbroken and Crushed"

The queen herself asked the same question. As she wrote to her Uncle Leopold:

The people of England viewed Albert as the queen's main source of support and assistance.

The poor fatherless baby of eight months is now the utterly heart-broken and crushed widow of forty-two! My *life* as a *happy* one is *ended*! The world is gone for *me*! . . . Oh! to be cut off in the prime of life—to see our pure, happy, quiet, domestic life, which *alone* enabled me to bear my *much* disliked position, CUT OFF at forty-two—when I *had* hoped with such instinctive certainty that God never *would* part us, and would let us grow old together (though *he* [Albert] always talked of the shortness of life)—is *too awful*, too cruel! [152]

She went on to tell her uncle this:

I am anxious to repeat *one* thing, and *that one* is *my firm* resolve, my *irrevocable decision*, viz., that *his* wishes—*his* plans—about everything, *his* views about *every* thing are to be *my law*! And *no human power* will make me swerve from *what he* decided and wished. . . . I am *also determined* that *no one* person— may *he* be ever so good, ever so devoted among my servants—is to lead or guide or dictate *to me*. I know *how he* would disapprove it. . . . Though miserably weak and utterly shattered, my spirit rises when I think *any* wish or plan of his is to be touched or changed, or I am to be *made* to do *anything*. [153]

At first Victoria vowed to continue her work as queen regardless of her loss, but within days she had changed her mind. She was in mourning. She couldn't possibly appear in public. She refused to meet with her ministers and wanted to stop all official duties.

Parliament felt she was being unreasonable. Although by now the powers of the monarchy had lessened dramatically, the queen still had many important things to do. In addition to attending diplomatic functions and public ceremonies, she had to keep advised of political events, study dispatches, sanction proposed legislation, sign documents, approve drafts of instructions and memorandums, write to dignitaries and ministers, and maintain a correspondence with other royals throughout the world.

Victoria's mail had always been excessive—on average she wrote twenty-five hundred words a day—but Prince Albert had handled many of the other duties for her. Now he was gone. Without her husband to advise her, the queen saw no point in meeting with her Cabinet. She suggested that Princess Alice go in her place.

But the members of the British government would not accept a substitute for their queen. They sympathized with her grief, but knew that the public expected a strong monarch. The privileges of royalty did not come without cost. At the very least, Victoria had to meet with her Cabinet members and stay informed on major issues. Otherwise, why have a monarch at all?

Parliament notified Victoria that it expected her to fulfill this particular obligation, and in the end she relented. But other than attending Cabinet meetings, she remained in seclusion. She shunned all public ceremonies and social events.

A Lengthy Mourning

By her own accounts, Victoria continued to grieve, to experience "those paroxysms of despair and yearning and longing and of daily, nightly longing to die," for three

Mourners gather at the funeral of Prince Albert. Albert's death plunged Victoria into a deep and long-lasting depression, causing her to write, "My life as a happy one is ended!"

full years.[154] During this time, she focused her attention on memorials for her late husband. She arranged for the publication of the prince's speeches and ordered a biography to be written about him. She constructed a mausoleum for him near Windsor. She unveiled statues of the prince in cities all over England, including the Albert Memorial near the site of her husband's Great Exhibition.

While Victoria was obsessed with preserving Albert's memory, her children suffered. They were not permitted to show any signs of happiness while in their mother's home. Alice's wedding to Prince Louis of Hesse and the Rhine, which was held on July 1, 1862, was as somber as a funeral. The next day the queen wrote to Vicky, who had missed the ceremony, "A dagger is plunged in my bleeding, desolate heart when I hear from (Alice) this morning that she is 'proud and happy' to be Louis's wife!"[155]

The younger children began to show signs of stress. Arthur, age twelve, who had sobbed at his father's funeral, still grieved. Leopold, age nine, became disobedient. At age five, Beatrice, always a happy, chattering child, became quiet and withdrawn.

A Mother's Wrath

Meanwhile, Bertie, now twenty-one, suffered from his mother's wrath. She blamed him for Albert's death. Though her husband had long been ill, in Victoria's mind, Bertie's love affair had delivered the fatal blow. When someone suggested that Bertie take over some of Albert's duties, Victoria stated that her son was "upon no account [to] be put at the head of any of those Societies or Commissions, or preside at any of those scientific proceedings, in which his beloved great Father took so prominent a part."[156]

When Bertie became engaged to Princess Alexandra of Denmark, his situation did not improve. The queen made it clear that she did not think him fit to rule England. Despite this, rumors spread that once Bertie married, the queen would abdicate her throne to him.

The wedding was scheduled for March 10, 1863. As the date approached, Victoria continued to mourn. By now Albert had

Queen Victoria had the Albert Memorial constructed as a tribute to her late husband. Similar memorials for Albert appeared throughout England.

The engagement of Bertie (left) to Princess Alexandra and the wedding of Alice (right) to Prince Louis greatly distressed Victoria, who found any displays of happiness after Albert's death inconceivable.

been dead over a year, and the British people felt it was time for the queen to resume her public duties. She never appeared in public except to unveil yet another statue of Prince Albert. Everyone was becoming irritated with her grief. As author Charles Dickens joked to a friend, "If you should meet with an inaccessible cave anywhere to which a hermit could re-

tire from the memory of Prince Albert and testimonials to the same, pray let me know of it. We have nothing solitary and deep enough in this part of England."[157]

British dressmakers, milliners, and hosiery manufacturers criticized the queen for continuing to wear black and forcing everyone in her household to do the same. They felt she was setting a bad example for British women, who often followed the fashions of the royal court and were not buying as much finery anymore. England had been somber for too long.

The Schleswig-Holstein Question

People were upset not only with the length of the queen's mourning period but with her outspoken opinion on what was known as the Schleswig-Holstein question. Schleswig and Holstein were two duchies currently under the control of Denmark. Neighboring Prussia felt it had a right to the territory, which was populated by Germans as well as Danes, and was threatening to invade it.

The British people were very sympathetic to little Denmark in its quarrel with the much larger Prussia. They viewed this struggle as similar to the biblical story of David and Goliath. They argued that England should help Denmark if war broke out, particularly because Bertie was marrying a Danish princess. But Victoria disagreed.

She had read some of Albert's papers that suggested Prussia had a rightful claim to the Schleswig-Holstein region. The queen firmly believed that if the prince were alive, he would be defending Prussia.

Unable to overcome her grief, Victoria (far right) dressed in black for several years after Albert's death.

Therefore, even though the rest of her family disagreed with her, she said Denmark was the transgressor.

Members of Parliament rebuked Victoria for favoring the Prussians. The queen in turn decided to convince the prime minister to share her view. On every possible occasion she badgered him with the idea that England should not support Denmark. He would not agree. After Prussia and Austria invaded Schleswig-Holstein, he proposed that England send warships to protect the Danish city of Copenhagen.

In the end, Parliament chose not to help Denmark, which then lost Schleswig-Holstein to Prussia and Austria. The British people largely blamed their queen. They could not believe that Victoria had sided with a country that in their opinion had behaved like a common bully. As a result, Victoria's popularity plummeted, and Bertie, who had sided with Denmark, was seen as a better leader. The public began stating openly what before had been said in whispers: Victoria should step down so that Bertie, the Prince of Wales, could be king.

9 Ruling an Empire

The day before Bertie's wedding to Princess Alexandra, Queen Victoria took him and his bride to Albert's mausoleum. There she announced that Albert had given the young couple his blessing. Victoria believed, as had her husband, that the soul lived on after death to watch over the living. She spoke of being separated from Prince Albert in body but not in spirit.

At the ceremony in St. George's Chapel, she remained solemn. She wore black and sat above everyone else in a private area called the Royal Closet. There she could be seen yet remain aloof. She told Vicky to make sure the few invited guests controlled their "noise and joyousness."[158] When the wedding was over, she avoided the luncheon held in the couple's honor. Instead she ate alone with daughter Beatrice, then visited Albert's mausoleum.

She wrote in her journal that evening:

All is over, and this (to me) most trying day is past, as a dream, for all seems like a dream now and leaves hardly any impression upon my poor mind and broken heart! Here I sit lonely and desolate, who so need love and tenderness, while our two daughters have each their loving husbands, and Bertie has taken his lovely, pure, sweet Bride

to Osbourne, such a jewel whom he is indeed lucky to have obtained.[159]

Later the queen wrote to Lord Palmerston about the event. She was distressed that her subjects had cheered the bridal

Though she was still in mourning for Albert, Queen Victoria approved of and attended the wedding of Bertie and Princess Alexandra (pictured).

procession on its way to the chapel. Though she was glad that they approved of the marriage, she said, "The Queen wishes Lord Palmerston would take an opportunity of stating the Queen's feeling on this great demonstration, but also to say that those err who think that the wound can be healed by the marriage of our child!"[160]

Now that he was married, Bertie hoped his mother would treat him more kindly. He was wrong. According to one British lord, in June 1863, there was

> much talk in London about the extraordinary way in which the Queen undertakes to direct the Prince and Princess of Wales in every detail of their lives. They may not dine out, except at houses named by her: nor ask anyone to dine with them, except with previous approval or unless the name of the person invited is on a list previously prepared: and the Princess, after

riding once or twice in the Park, was forbidden to do so again.[161]

Queen Victoria felt that she could completely control the heir to the throne, but her power over her son turned out to be as limited as her power over Parliament. Bertie responded to his mother's restrictions by visiting the racetrack, gambling, smoking, partying, and associating with people that the queen considered to be disreputable, such as all Americans and anyone who practiced the Jewish religion. Bertie's wife, too, indulged in activities that Victoria regarded as unacceptable, such as sleeping until 11 A.M. every morning and knitting in public.

However, the queen did not entirely blame the prince and princess for their bad habits. She felt that they were basically good people whose weak characters had allowed them to be influenced by society. Victoria believed that the world was becoming too loose in its morals. She railed

Condolences to Mrs. Lincoln

In this letter dated April 29, 1865, and quoted in Hibbert's Queen Victoria in Her Letters and Journals, *Victoria wrote her condolences to Mrs. Abraham Lincoln, whose husband had just been assassinated.*

"Though a stranger to you, I cannot remain silent when so terrible a calamity has fallen upon you and your country, and must express personally my deep and heartfelt sympathy with you under the shocking circumstances of your present dreadful misfortune.

No one can better appreciate than I can, who am myself utterly brokenhearted by the loss of my own beloved husband, who was the light of my life, my stay, my all, what your sufferings must be; and I earnestly pray that you may be supported by Him to Whom alone the sorely stricken can look for comfort, in this hour of heavy affliction!"

against the irresponsible behavior of British youth as a whole.

Meanwhile, the public blamed Victoria for Bertie's unsavory pastimes. Newspaper articles describing his escapades often pointed out that the queen did not give her son enough to do. Although she allowed Bertie to appear at a few ceremonies, she did not permit him to handle any of her official duties. Therefore, instead of believing that the future King Edward VII was unfit to rule, people felt that he deserved more responsibility. Many said that Queen Victoria should relinquish her throne to him immediately.

Still in Seclusion

Talk of Victoria's abdication increased as she remained in seclusion. On the third anniversary of Albert's death, the queen was still in mourning. She failed to appear at many important functions and refused to receive foreign visitors. On one occasion, she insisted that the king and queen of Denmark stay at a hotel when she should have invited them to be guests in the royal residence.

The public was truly angry. One editorial in the *Times* stated:

> The living have their claims as well as the dead; and what claims can be more important than those of a great nation, and the Society of one of the first European Capitals? The Queen should think of her subjects' claims and the duties of her high station, and not postpone them longer to the indulgence of an unavailing grief . . . [it was] impossible for a recluse to occupy the British

Victoria was often criticized by the media for treating her son Bertie poorly. Here, a cartoon pokes fun at one of Bertie's visits, in which the queen has banished him to a corner.

throne without a gradual weakening of that authority which the Sovereign has been accustomed to exert.[162]

Other newspaper reports were more humorous. On April 1, 1864, the *Times* published this announcement as an April Fools' Day joke: "Her Majesty's loyal subjects will be very pleased to hear that their Sovereign is about to break her protracted seclusion." The month before, someone had put a sign on Buckingham Palace stating, "These commanding premises to be

Victoria sits atop a horse led by her servant John Brown. Brown's straightforward manner helped to bring the queen out of her protracted depression.

let or sold, in consequence of the late occupant's declining business."[163]

Clearly the queen could not remain in hiding any longer. Friends and family tried to convince her to end her mourning. Her Uncle Leopold warned, "The English are very personal; to continue to love people they must see them."[164] Victoria did not want to listen.

The Queen and John Brown

Then Dr. William Jenner, the royal physician, had an idea. He knew that Victoria had spoken highly of a man named John Brown, the groom at her stables in Scotland. Jenner sent for Brown, then told Vic-

toria she needed to start horseback riding again for her health. He hoped Brown would be able to bring the queen out of her depression. He was right.

Within weeks, she was quoting the thirty-nine-year-old Brown in her journal. On February 3, 1865, she wrote, "Have decided that Brown should remain permanently & make himself useful in other ways besides leading my pony as he is so very dependable."[165] She decreed that he was "The Queen's Highland Servant" and ordered that he was to accompany her "ALWAYS and everywhere out of doors, whether riding or driving or on foot; and it is a *real* comfort, for he is *so* devoted to me—so simple, so intelligent, so unlike an *ordinary* servant, and so cheerful and attentive."[166]

Brown was a handsome Scotsman with a direct way of speaking to the queen. "Hoots, wumman, canna ye hold yer head still!" he said, while trying to pin a shawl around her shoulders. "What's this ye've got on today?"[167] he'd ask if she was wearing something he didn't like. Victoria enjoyed his straightforward manner, and as time went on, she depended on him more and more.

"My nature is too passionate, my emotions too fervent," she once wrote after Albert's death, "and I am a person who has to cling to some one in order to find peace and comfort."[168] John Brown had become that someone.

But other people were not so fond of Brown. They found him arrogant and rude. He got into fights and sometimes drank heavily. Victoria's children were appalled that she had given so much power to a former stable boy. As Princess Alice explained, "He alone talks to her on all things, while we, her children, are restricted to speak on only those matters which do not excite her, or of which she chooses to talk."[169]

The rest of the household was equally unhappy with Brown. Victoria's longtime servants resented this newcomer. They were jealous of his position and the many gifts he received.

The public did not care for Brown either. They gossiped about his relationship to the queen and called Victoria "Mrs. Brown." One visiting American recounted just how out of hand the rumors were becoming.

NO SMOKING

According to Barry St. John Nevill, writing in Life at the Court of Queen Victoria, 1861–1901, *the widowed queen found smoking distasteful and did everything she could to discourage the habit in her presence.*

"The Queen made smokers go into the garden if they wished to smoke at Osbourne House and when Prince Christian was courting her daughter, Princess Helena, she provided him with a damp, white-washed room near the servants' quarters. She had 'NO SMOKING' notices placed almost everywhere in her homes and when King Albert of Saxony visited her, he was warned about smoking. He was a heavy smoker and it was only with great difficulty that he managed to do without a cigar for two days. On the third day he remembered that he was a king and so walked up the grand staircase puffing a large cigar, which he said gave him great satisfaction. But it is reported that it deeply shocked those courtiers who witnessed it."

I have been told that the Queen was insane, and John Brown was her keeper; that the Queen was a spiritualist and John Brown was her medium—in a word, a hundred stories, each more absurd than the other, and all vouched for by men of considerable station and authority.[170]

The queen fueled these rumors by spending much of her time riding alone with John Brown in his beloved Scottish Highlands. In 1868 she published a book entitled *Leaves from the Journal of My Life in the Highlands*; within three months 100,000 copies were sold. It described her days with Albert at Balmoral, but because she spoke of the Highlanders with such affection it reminded people of Brown. One book reviewer noted "that it is only with *Scottish servants* one could be on such blessed terms."[171]

Few seemed to appreciate that Brown was slowly bringing the queen out of her depression. By mid-1864 she was venturing out in public again, riding through London in an open carriage. The following year, on the anniversary of her late husband's birthday, she attended a colorful ceremony in his honor, and in 1866 she went to several official functions, even making a speech at one of them. She also opened Parliament for the first time since Albert's death.

The public still did not think Queen Victoria was doing enough. In fact, they suspected that John Brown was really ruling the country. Rumors spread that the queen had secretly married him and borne his child. Cartoons appeared mocking the relationship between Victoria and her Highland servant. One showed a Scotsman leaning against the British throne, a lion at his feet.

Disraeli and Gladstone

Despite public opinion, it was the queen and not John Brown who signed official documents and dealt with the prime minister. Lord Palmerston had died in 1865 and been replaced by a succession of men. In February 1868 Benjamin Disraeli became prime minister. Disraeli complimented the queen. "He is full of poetry, romance & chivalry," she wrote in her journal. "When he knelt down to kiss my hand [which] he took in both his—he said: 'In loving loyalty & faith.'"[172]

Victoria responded to Disraeli's attentions by giving him her complete confi-

Prime Minister Benjamin Disraeli won the favor of the queen, who often accepted his advice on important issues.

The election of William Gladstone as prime minister disappointed the queen, who disagreed with many of Gladstone's positions and refused to open Parliament for him.

the Fenians. They were using violence as a form of protest and had threatened to kill Queen Victoria.

Religion was one source of Irish anger. Most people in Ireland were Roman Catholic. However, the Protestant British government had established the Anglican Church there and taxed the Irish to support it. Gladstone reasoned that Great Britain could calm the Irish by disestablishing the Anglican Church. Queen Victoria disagreed.

She also disagreed with Gladstone's suggestion that Bertie should take up part-time residence in Ireland and become its viceroy. She had already made her opinion on this matter clear to Disraeli. "*Any encouragement* of [Bertie's] constant love of running about, and not keeping at home or near the Queen, is *earnestly* and *seriously* to be depreciated."[173] She told Gladstone that she would not discuss the Prince of Wales with him.

dence. Often he could persuade her to change her mind on important issues. Victoria enjoyed his company and hoped he would remain prime minister for a long time.

She was soon disappointed. Nine months after taking office, Disraeli was defeated at a general election, and William Gladstone became the new prime minister.

Victoria disagreed with Gladstone on many issues. She particularly disliked his views on Ireland, which no longer wanted to be ruled by England. Some Irishmen had formed an anti-British group called

The Queen's Stubbornness

She also declined to open Parliament for him. Her traditional appearance at this official ceremony, marking the start of a new government session, was important, but Victoria said she could not possibly attend because she was in poor health. Said one observer:

I believe that neither health and strength are wanting, were [her] inclination what it should be. It is simply the long, unchecked habit of self-indulgence that now makes it impossible for her, without some degree of nervous agitation, to give up, even for ten minutes, the gratification of a single inclination, or even *whim*.[174]

In other words, Victoria wasn't really sick. She just didn't want to do anything she didn't have to.

Disraeli was worried. According to one friend, he thought that

> the monarchy was in danger, which he never did before: not from immediate causes, nor from any feeling against it of a strongly hostile character, but from gradual loss of prestige; the Queen has thrown away her chances, people find out that they can do without a Court, etc.[175]

In other words, by now the British public believed that their queen did absolutely nothing, and that despite her inactivity, the government continued to function smoothly. Therefore, many argued that a monarch was completely unnecessary, especially given the expense of supporting one. It wasn't that people were particularly hostile towards Victoria or her behavior. They simply didn't think she was worth keeping.

Despite public opinion, Victoria continued to avoid her duties. In February 1870 she again refused to open Parliament. Later that year, Gladstone wrote about the "Royalty question" to Lord Granville, saying, "To speak in rude and

Jack the Ripper

When the notorious "Jack the Ripper" murders occurred, many people offered the police advice on how to catch the killer. Victoria was no exception, as shown by this letter she wrote to England's home secretary, as quoted in Hibbert's Queen Victoria in Her Letters and Journals.

"The Queen fears that the detective department is not so efficient as it might be. No doubt the recent murders in Whitechapel were committed in circumstances which made detection very difficult; still, the Queen thinks that, in the small area where these horrible crimes have been perpetrated, a great number of detectives might be employed, and that every possible suggestion might be carefully examined and, if practicable, followed.

Have the cattle boats and passenger boats been examined?

Has any investigation been made as to the number of single men occupying rooms to themselves?

The murderer's clothes must be saturated with blood and must be kept somewhere.

Is there sufficient surveillance at night?

These are some of the questions that occur to the Queen on reading the accounts of this horrible crime."

Victoria, shown at the opening of Parliament, was criticized by her subjects for acting only when she needed money.

general terms, the Queen is invisible and the Prince of Wales is not respected."[176]

Victoria Asks for Money

Then Victoria realized she needed money to pay for daughter Louise's wedding. In addition, her son Arthur was turning eighteen and required an increase in his allowance. Victoria wanted the British government to approve these expenditures, so in an attempt to gain their favor she agreed to open Parliament in February 1871.

Her subjects were furious. It seemed as though Victoria acted only when she wanted more money. They felt she already received enough. The nation paid her a substantial allowance, in addition to providing for the maintainance of Windsor Castle, Buckingham Palace, the royal yacht, her guards, her horses, and countless other expenses. In addition, all nine of the queen's children received allowances from the government, as did her numerous grandchildren. By this time,

Bertie was the father of six. Where would it all end? The Britons looked at France's recently formed republic and wondered whether their monarchy should continue.

Victoria protested that her seclusion was due to her poor health. Yet people reported that she looked quite fit while on vacation both at Osbourne and at Balmoral. In the Highlands she had climbed the steep Craig Gowan. But she wrote Gladstone that at fifty-two she was "a woman no longer young" who could not "be driven and abused till her nerves and health will give way with the worry and agitation and interference in her private life."[177] She said she would rather abdicate the throne than be overworked to death.

A Serious Illness

Suddenly the queen really did fall seriously ill. She had a throat abscess and swelling under one arm. In addition, she developed gout, a disease that causes swelling of the feet and hands. Newspapers at last expressed some concern. In September 1871, Disraeli made a speech in which he stated that the queen had been "morally and physically incapacitated"[178] for quite some time. Opponents seized on this phrase, using it to argue that the queen had long been unfit to rule.

Then in November the Prince of Wales came down with typhoid fever. The nation was shocked. As Bertie hovered near death, people remembered that Prince Albert had died exactly ten years before from, they incorrectly believed, the very same disease. All over Great Britain, Queen Victoria's subjects said prayers for her son's recovery. Newspapers put out special editions to report on the progress of his condition. Finally Bertie began to improve.

By February he was well enough to attend a public thanksgiving service in his honor. Held at St. Paul's Cathedral, the ceremony drew cheering crowds. Two days later, after a member of the Irish Fenians waved an unloaded pistol at Victoria, the British people realized how much they valued their queen. The monarchy was popular again.

Chapter

10 Beloved Queen

Now Queen Victoria was free to do as she pleased without fear of public opinion. Although she continued to sign documents and meet with Prime Minister Gladstone, she vacationed at Balmoral or Osbourne for many months at a time.

Then in 1874, Disraeli replaced Gladstone, and Victoria's interest in politics increased. Once again she greatly enjoyed the company of her prime minister, who, in an effort to please the queen, used his influence to induce Parliament to pass any laws she proposed.

One of the laws Victoria suggested was the Public Worship Act, designed to end certain practices in the Catholic religion that originated in Rome. She specifically wanted to eliminate confession and what

Disraeli, shown addressing the House of Commons, used his influence to help pass any laws that the queen proposed.

she called "bowings and scrapings."[179] At the time, such activities were termed *ritualism.* Queen Victoria was afraid that if ritualism was left unchecked, it would spread and threaten what she considered to be the country's true religion, Protestantism. Disraeli personally disagreed with the Public Worship Act; nevertheless, he helped persuade Parliament to pass it.

Another one of Victoria's proposed laws involved animal rights. All her life she had enjoyed the company of her many dogs. In 1876 she convinced Disraeli to push the Vivisection Bill into law. It required that all animals used for research purposes be treated humanely.

Even more important to Victoria was the Royal Titles Act. Since India was under British rule, Victoria had long ago decided she should be called its empress. The Royal Titles Act would officially give her that name. Under Disraeli's influence, the act became law in 1876, when Parliament declared that the queen of England was also the empress of India.

With Disraeli's Parliament acting on so many of her recommendations, Victoria's self-confidence soared. In earlier years, as Albert's wife, she had often echoed the opinions of her husband. Now she voiced more and more of her own. No longer in Prince Albert's shadow, she was once again the independent woman she had been at the beginning of her reign.

Yet she did not support Britain's growing feminist movement. In fact, the queen said women's rights were "dangerous, and unchristian and unnatural." She once told Gladstone, "The Queen is a woman herself and knows what an anomaly her own position is . . . let women be what God intended; a helpmate for a man—but with totally different duties and vocations."[180]

The Spiritual and Material Worlds

Victoria offers advice to her daughter Princess Victoria of Hesse in a letter dated August 22, 1883, and quoted in Hibbert's Queen Victoria in Her Letters and Journals.

"There is one thing which I had wished to speak to you about but had no opportunity of doing so, and that is: that I would earnestly warn you against trying to find out the reason for and explanation of everything.

Science can explain many things, but there is a spiritual as well as a material World and this former cannot be explained. We must have faith and trust, and believe in all ruling, all wise and benificent Providence which orders all things. To try and find out the reason for everything is very dangerous and leads to nothing but disappointment and dissatisfaction, unsettling your mind and in the end making you miserable."

She particularly spoke out against women becoming doctors instead of nurses.

A New Generation

The queen's daughters considered their mother's views to be old-fashioned. Vicky, Alice, and Louise all favored women's rights. Louise, who had married a member of Parliament rather than a prince like the rest of her sisters, wrote feminist articles under the pseudonym "Mira Fontenoy." An artist and member of the Royal Society of Painters and Etchers, she also rode bicycles, smoked cigars, and had eccentric friends. She and Vicky both maintained an ongoing correspondence with Josephine Butler, a well-known social reformer.

Meanwhile, their sister Helena was occupying herself with quieter pursuits. She founded a needlework school and held charity bazaars. Her husband, the exiled, penniless Prince Christian of Schleswig-Holstein, was the ranger of Windsor Park. Victoria was pleased that the young couple lived nearby. In fact, she had chosen Christian for Helena specifically because he had no home of his own, and she knew the young couple would have to stay in England and depend on her support.

For son Affie the queen wanted a wife who had dark eyes, believing "that constant fair hair and blue eyes makes the blood so lymphatic."[181] She remembered that her husband had once said that to keep the royal line healthy, "We must have some strong, dark blood"[182] for a change. To this end, she asked Vicky to help her find a suitable mate for Affie.

But Affie did not want his mother to choose a bride for him. He chose one

Victoria made certain that Princess Helena (pictured) would live nearby and remain dependent on her by choosing a penniless prince as Helena's husband.

himself, the Grand Duchess Marie of Russia. Victoria was upset. She disliked the Russians. When her daughter Alice spoke up in Marie's defense, the queen wrote:

> You have *entirely* taken the Russian side, & I do *not* think, dear Child, that *you* should tell *me* who have been nearly 20 *years longer* on the throne than the Emperor of Russia & am the Doyenne of Sovereigns & who am a *Reigning* Sovereign which the Empress is not,—*what I ought to do.* I think I know *that.*[183]

Despite Victoria's opposition, Affie and Marie were married in January 1874. Five years later, his brother Arthur married Princess Louise Margaret of Prussia. Her parents were estranged, and Victoria believed that Arthur, her favorite son, was marrying the girl because he felt sorry for her. Nonetheless, she approved of the match.

Three months before Arthur's wedding, his sister Alice and Alice's youngest child, May, both died from diphtheria. Victoria sent a governess to care for the surviving children and remained in touch with the eldest, her namesake, for years.

Another death occurred in 1884, when Victoria's son Leopold finally succumbed to his disease. He had been sickly his whole life, yet he had been strong willed, too. On one occasion, claiming an "intense aversion" to Balmoral, he went to Paris instead of joining the royal family vacation in the Highlands. Victoria accused him of going against the "authority of the Sovereign and the Throne" and said, "He must be made to feel that such conduct cannot be tolerated."[184]

Leopold also married against his mother's wishes. Victoria had always felt that Leopold was too ill to become anyone's husband. "No one knows the constant fear I am in about him,"[185] she wrote. But in 1882 he wed Princess Helen of Waldeck-Pyrmont. Upon his death two years later he left behind two children.

The year after Leopold's death, Victoria's youngest child, Beatrice, married Prince Henry ("Liko") of Battenberg. This union, too, went against the queen's wishes. She hadn't wanted Beatrice to marry anybody at all, preferring Baby to remain at home with her. Mother and daughter fought over the issue. Finally, Victoria

gave her permission for the marriage, but she made Beatrice promise to remain in England and work as her private secretary.

The wedding was a simple affair. It was the first royal wedding performed in a small parish church with only a few guests present. Notably, Victoria's daughter Vicky and her husband refused to attend. They and other Prussian and Russian relatives felt that the Battenbergs were not highborn enough to marry into the royal family. Vicky's husband Fritz had been particularly outspoken about his displeasure with Beatrice's choice of husband.

The queen angrily defended her new son-in-law, whose company she greatly enjoyed. She found him to be a cheerful, entertaining man and was delighted when Beatrice gave birth to his son in 1886. Queen Victoria was the first in the family to hold the new baby. She had been present during his birth, as she was with as many of her grandchildren as possible.

Ever-Changing Prime Ministers

While Victoria was dealing with her grown children, she was also coping with a changing government. In 1880, Prime Minister Disraeli again lost his position to Gladstone, who then lost it to the marquess of Salisbury five years later. Salisbury held on as prime minister for only a year before Gladstone again took over, only to be defeated a few months later in favor of Salisbury again. For the next several years, the two men would continue to fight for control of Parliament.

Victoria found these transitions difficult, particularly because Disraeli, Gladstone, and Salisbury were so different from one another. She got along best with Disraeli. "He had a way when we differed . . .," she commented, "of saying 'Dear Madam' so persuasively, and putting his head on one side."[186] He completely charmed her and avoided explosive conflict. As Disraeli himself explained, "I never contradict, I never deny; but I sometimes forget."[187]

He became Victoria's favorite minister, in part because he offered her excessive praise. "Everyone likes flattery," he once told a friend, "and when you come to royalty you should lay it on with a trowel."[188] He also kept the queen informed on all the latest gossip. According to one royal observer, every day Disraeli wrote Victoria long, flowery letters, in which he told her "every scrap of political news dressed up to serve his own purpose, and every scrap of social gossip cooked to amuse her."[189]

Still, his devotion to the queen was sincere. He genuinely enjoyed her company, and generally got along well with women. "I owe everything to women," he said, "and if in the sunset of my life I have still a young heart, it is due to that influence."[190] Disraeli liked to refer to Victoria as "The Faerie Queen," a reference to a famous epic poem written in the late 1500s by Edmund Spenser. *The Faerie Queene* describes a land filled with adventure, magic, and monsters where a loyal knight serves the queen of all faeries and elves.

When Disraeli left office in 1880, Victoria wrote to him, "What your loss to me as a Minister would be, it is impossible to estimate. But I trust you will always remain my friend, to whom I can turn and on whom I can rely."[191] A year later, when he died of bronchitis, she noted, "Never had I *so* kind and devoted a Minister and very few such devoted friends."[192]

In contrast, Victoria disliked Gladstone and was upset whenever he controlled Parliament. Although this prime minister treated her with the utmost courtesy and respect, she found him too formal and stiff. "He speaks to me as if I were a public meeting,"[193] she supposedly complained.

She also continued to disagree with Gladstone's outspoken opinions on how the government and military should be run. Upon his death in 1898, she wrote, "He was very clever and full of ideas for bettering the advancement of the country, always most loyal to me personally, and ready to do anything for the Royal Family; but alas! I am sure involuntarily, he did at times a good deal of harm."[194]

With Prime Minister Salisbury, Victoria had another kind of relationship. At age fifty-five, he was the first prime minister to be younger than the queen. As a boy he had been a page at her coronation. She trusted him and continued to correspond with him even when he was not in office, sending him copies of official letters and documents. She was particularly pleased that he shared her opinions on British expansionism. Victoria believed that Great Britain should actively expand its rule throughout the world, thereby becoming a true empire. She wanted her forces to occupy not only India but Africa as well.

Wars Abroad

Out of this expansionist policy came several wars. Fighting broke out in Egypt as Great Britain tried to retain control of the Suez Canal. In South Africa the native

Prime Minister Salisbury shared the queen's desire to expand British rule throughout the world.

Zulus battled British occupation, as did the Boers, who were Dutch settlers in the region. The Boer War lasted from 1899 to 1902 and cost many lives.

As Great Britain's influence spread to China, Samoa, and elsewhere, Queen Victoria began to doubt the policy of expansionism. She was concerned that England's desire to control as much territory as possible made it risk the anger of other countries, such as Germany, that wanted the same territory. She said she "could not quite understand why nobody was to have anything anywhere but ourselves."[195] Still, she defended the policy in arguments with her grandson William, Vicky's eldest child, who was now the German emperor, Kaiser Wilhelm II.

"Poor Good Munshi"

Meanwhile, Victoria still enjoyed her position as empress of India. By the late 1800s she had imported several Indian servants and chosen one of them, twenty-four-year-old Abdul Karim, as her personal favorite. Realizing that Karim was very smart, she hired someone to tutor him in English, and he in turn began to teach her his language, Hindustani. Soon Victoria was calling him "Munshi," which meant "teacher."

The queen eventually made Munshi her official Indian secretary. This upset many in her Cabinet. They wrote the queen that Munshi's background was not appropriate for such a high position. She replied:

> To make out that the poor good Munshi is so *low* is really *outrageous* & in a country like England quite out of place. . . . She has known 2 Archbishops who were sons respectively of a Butcher & a Grocer. . . . Abdul's father saw good & honourable service as a Dr & he [Abdul] feels cut to the heart at being thus spoken of. It probably comes from some low jealous Indians or Anglo-Indians. . . . The Queen is so sorry for the poor Munshi's sensitive feelings.[196]

Earlier Victoria had written of "her very strong feeling (and she has few stronger) that the natives and coloured races should be treated with every kindness and affection, as brothers, not—as alas! Englishmen too often do!—as totally different beings to ourselves, fit only to be crushed and shot down!" [197] This opinion was very different from the prevailing view of her subjects, who believed that anyone with darker skin was inferior. By giving Munshi such a powerful role in her life, Victoria was setting an important example for people everywhere.

The Jubilees

The queen ignored all objections that she treated Indians and Africans too well, and she invited them to be honored guests at her jubilee celebrations. The Golden Jubilee in 1887 and the Diamond Jubilee in 1897 marked the fiftieth and sixtieth anniversaries of Victoria's reign. They were spectacular symbols of her monarchy.

George Gissing wrote about the Golden Jubilee in his contemporary, popular novel *In the Year of Jubilee*. The festivities were

to celebrate the fiftieth year of the reign of Queen Victoria—yes; but at the same time, and far more, it's to celebrate the completion of fifty years of Progress. National Progress without precedent in the history of mankind! One may say, indeed, Progress of the Human Race. Only think what has

Victoria decorates an officer for merit in the Afghan and Zulu wars.

The queen is honored at the 1897 Diamond Jubilee, a grand celebration that marked the sixtieth anniversary of her reign.

been done in this half-century; only think of it! Compare England now, compare the world with what it was in 1837. It takes away one's breath![198]

The jubilees have also been credited with ushering in the age of consumerism, for they marked the first time that mass-produced souvenirs appeared to commemorate an event. Queen Victoria's picture graced mugs, flags, plates, dishes, handkerchiefs, boxes of chocolate, and countless other items for sale everywhere. At the Golden Jubilee, every schoolchild was given a free souvenir mug. More than thirty thousand children enjoyed games and other entertainment in Hyde Park, and millions of people watched a royal procession that included the queen, two of her daughters, and the royal princes.

Many, many poems were written in the queen's honor. The verse of one woman, Clara Thwaites, was typical of the tributes:

O sons, brave sons, so stalwart, true and free,
O daughters fair—a Woman's jubilee,
A Sovereign's glad, imperial decree
Calls with a clarion tongue, "Rejoice with me!"[199]

By the time of her Diamond Jubilee in 1897, Victoria had reigned longer than any other English king or queen. The festivities were even grander than they had been ten years earlier. As she traveled through her kingdom, "the streets, the windows, the roofs of the houses, were one mass of beaming faces, and the cheers never ceased," and she received so many telegrams that "it was quite impossible to open them."[200]

A thanksgiving service was held in her honor at St. Paul's Cathedral. At age seventy-eight, Victoria's legs were too feeble to allow her to climb the steps, so she remained outside in her carriage. According to her daughter Vicky, "the scene in front of St. Paul's was most impressive, and when the bells pealed out from the dark old cathedral, and the cheers rang out again, and the sun shone on all the glitter of the escort and carriages, it was as fine a sight as you could wish to see."[201]

Setting a Good Example

Jubilee biographies extolled the many virtues of the queen's life. To her delight, she was said to have set a good example for her subjects. Victoria wanted to believe that her behavior had indeed influenced people. In the past, she had seen women copy the fashions she wore. Now she hoped that at least some of them also copied her behavior.

The queen had long been concerned about declining morals. In a letter to Vicky in 1877, she wrote that engaged couples had

lost all modesty for not only do they go about driving, walking, and visiting—everywhere alone, they have also now taken to go out everywhere together in society—which till a year or so no young lady just engaged, ever did, and make a regular show of themselves and are laughed at and stared at! In short young people are getting very American, I fear in their views and ways.[202]

Victoria Mentions Resignation

In 1885 Parliament recalled troops that were fighting to reclaim British territory in Africa. In this letter from Hibbert's Queen Victoria in Her Letters and Journals, *Victoria tells the secretary of war how upset she is over her government's decision.*

"As the present Government seem to act entirely according to the dictates of Parliament irrespective of any settled policy, Parliament should be told the truth and at once. . . .

To see her brave soldiers as the Queen did yesterday gashed and mutilated for nothing is dreadful! And to see for the second time our troops recalled and retreating before savages—probably and most probably only to have to send them out again in a little while—is to make us the laughing-stock of the world! For military reasons the strongly expressed opinion of the Generals should be listened to!

The Queen writes strongly, but she cannot resign if matters go ill, and her heart bleeds to see such short-sighted humiliating policy pursued, which lowers her country before the whole world."

Victoria had condemned gambling and other vices long before Bertie had taken them up. Now she continued to chastise her children and grandchildren whenever they behaved badly. Even though she once said, "I feel very deeply that my opinion and my advice are never listened to and that it is almost useless to give any,"[203] she spoke against irresponsible behavior at every opportunity.

Because of her strong code of proper behavior, she was considered a model British mother. One verse in the official "Jubilee Song" said, "Let ev'ry English Maiden make this her frequent prayer; That she the same high purpose may with her Sovereign share."[204] People admired her commitment to virtue.

They also applauded her efforts to improve housing for the poor. In 1883 Victoria read a pamphlet entitled "The Bitter Outcry of Outcast London" by the Reverend Andrew Mearns, which described the deplorable condition of British slums. It reminded her of her husband's desire to improve the lives of the poor, and she realized that she had not done enough to honor his vision for England. She pressed

Victoria is surrounded by family members as she tours the 1891 Royal Navy exhibit. Considered a model British mother by her subjects, the queen remained close to her family throughout her life.

The Keenest Interest in Death

In this excerpt from an April 1890 letter to her family, as quoted in Victor Mallet's Life with Queen Victoria: Marie Mallet's Letters from Court 1887–1901, *lady-in-waiting Marie Mallet describes Victoria's reaction to the death of one of her housemaids.*

"It is very curious to see how the Queen takes the keenest interest in death and all its horrors, our whole talk has been of coffins and winding sheets. We had a sort of funeral service last night in the Dining Room, the coffin in our midst not even screwed down, everyone in evening dress, the servants sobbing; it was too dreadful and got upon my nerves to such an extent that I never slept all night. The Queen was very grieved and placed a wreath on the coffin rather tremblingly; and then the body was removed to the little English church close by and this afternoon we had to visit it again with the Queen. The final funeral is tomorrow and after that we may hope for a little peace. Of course I admire the Queen for taking such a lively interest in her servants, but it is overdone in this sort of way and it is very trying for the Household."

government officials to create an organization that would examine sanitary conditions throughout the poorer sections of large towns. Her efforts helped establish the Royal Commission on Housing in 1884.

In other ways, too, Victoria used her memories of the past to improve the future, and Albert wasn't her only influence. For example, she recalled Florence Nightingale's efforts to improve hospital facilities during the Crimean War and decided that the hospitals in India needed similar help. She sent British physicians to India to introduce modern medical techniques.

Her involvement in charitable causes only heightened Victoria's popularity. By now she was well loved; consequently the monarchy system remained strong. Because of Victoria's long reign, many people had known no other ruler. They accepted the current form of government without complaint, and in fact they felt like they were members of Victoria's family. Wrote biographer Giles St. Aubyn:

No previous British Sovereign was anything like so well known as Queen Victoria. The invention of photography, the coming of the railway, and the rapid growth of literacy, combined to spread her fame. State education also played a part in adding to her prestige. Not a schoolday began without saying a prayer for the Queen and the Royal Family.[205]

Her death in January 1901, therefore, sent the entire British empire into shock. Victoria had been ill for quite some

Crimean War veterans present Victoria with a bouquet of flowers at a reception held in the south of France.

time—she suffered from rheumatism, indigestion, insomnia, and failing vision—but no one expected her to die. It seemed as though she would go on forever.

Victoria's Last Days

She had spent her last years mostly at Balmoral or Osbourne, enjoying literature, theatrical performances, and the simple pleasures of the countryside. As one of her ladies-in-waiting wrote from Balmoral:

> Putting grumbling aside the life here is utterly dull, we see nothing of the Queen except at dinner on alternate nights, we have *no* duties to perform to occupy our minds and the weather is horribly cold and wet. At the same time it is impossible to settle to anything on account of interruptions. We just exist from meal to meal and do our best to kill time.[206]

Then the inevitable happened. At Osbourne on the morning of Wednesday, January 16, 1901, the queen had trouble awakening. The day before, she had gone for a drive with a visiting friend, and now she seemed dazed and confused. Her doctor feared she had suffered a stroke. He telegraphed family members, and soon

Victoria's children and grandchildren were rushing to her side. Bertie issued a public statement on January 19, 1901:

> The Queen has not lately been in her usual health, and is unable for the present to take her customary drives. The Queen during the past year has had a great strain upon her powers, which has rather told upon Her Majesty's nervous system. It has, therefore, been thought advisable by Her Majesty's physicians that the Queen should be kept perfectly quiet in the house, and should abstain for the present from transacting business.[207]

For a time Victoria seemed better, but occasionally she would slip into confusion again. At one point she asked for her favorite dog to be placed in bed with her. She received visitors, including Kaiser Wilhelm, who remained by her side for hours. "I don't want to die yet," she said. "There are several things I want to arrange."[208]

Then, suddenly, she looked out her bedroom window, called out Albert's name, and died. Wrote Princess Helena, "I shall never forget the look of radiance on her face. . . . One *felt* and knew she saw beyond the Border Land—and had *seen* and *met* all *her loved ones.* In death she was so beautiful, such peace and joy on her dear face—a radiance from Heaven."[209]

From that moment on, Queen Victoria became a treasured memory for the British people. Tributes to her abounded; few dared criticize her. She had become a symbol of British stability and greatness.

But above all she was a human being. "In after years," she had earlier written, "God would not distinguish between the good life of a Crowned head or a peasant."[210] According to biographer Elizabeth Longford, Victoria

> would be judged along with the humblest of her people—the poor heedless Irish, the innocent Africans, the faithful Indians, the old Highland women hidden away in dark cupboard-beds, or the London mob. The most that she and any of them could hope to plead was that they had tried to be good.[211]

Through her countless letters and journal entries, Victoria left behind a portrait of a woman who did indeed try to be good. She struggled to balance work and family without giving up those values that were important to her. As a result, the Victorian age has come to represent conservative morality and righteous living. Queen Victoria was nothing if not a virtuous woman.

Because of this, Victoria has often been credited with saving the British monarchy. Her predecessors had been so ill mannered and corrupt that their subjects spoke of overthrowing the government and starting a democracy. In contrast, Victoria was a sovereign in whom the people of Great Britain could take pride. They viewed her as the matriarch of an extended global family that included many countries never before under British rule.

A Global Influence

Queen Victoria's influence was felt around the world. Her empire included parts of Asia and Africa, and her navy explored the Arctic Circle. Her life was significant to millions of people at home and abroad, and her children and grandchildren would go on to make their own marks on history.

But above all, Queen Victoria teaches a lesson for modern times. According to biographer Longford, during Victoria's reign people developed a strong belief in improvement. They wanted to better themselves and the world. Perhaps they acquired this attitude from their queen.

Victoria led what could be called an examined life. In other words, she did not make decisions without careful thought, nor did she dismiss mistakes without analyzing them. Her journal writings were a way for her to keep in touch with her deepest feelings. As a result, she remained true to her beliefs. Her viewpoints did not depend on the whims of public opinion. This constancy made her subjects feel very secure. They could trust their queen to remain the same throughout the years.

This stability was important during an era of upheaval. Modern society was facing an amazing array of advances in science, medicine, and technology. It was difficult for people to absorb so many new ideas, and it was comforting to have the same, steady, reliable monarch presiding over it all.

Victoria listens as her daughter Beatrice reads her the day's news. Even at the end of her long reign, Victoria remained true to her values, serving as a role model for people throughout the world.

In fact, Queen Victoria's most significant contribution was not a specific accomplishment; it was her ongoing, lasting influence on the monarchy system itself. As noted scholars Sir Edgar Trevor Williams and Meredith Veldman explain in their article "Victoria and the Victorian Age," by the end of her life

[Queen Victoria] had made the monarchy respectable and had thereby guaranteed its continuance—not as a political power but as a political institution. Her long reign had woven a legend, and, as her political power ebbed away, her political value grew. It lay, perhaps, more in what the electorate thought of her, indeed felt about her, than in what she ever was or certainly ever believed herself to be. [212]

They later add:

[Victoria's] essential achievement was simple. By the length of her reign, the longest in English history, she had restored both dignity and popularity to a tarnished crown: an achievement of character, as well as of longevity. Historians may differ in their assessment of her political acumen, her political importance, or her role as a constitutional monarch. None will question her high sense of duty or the transparent honesty, the massive simplicity, of her royal character. [213]

In the end, what was most important about Queen Victoria was the way she remained true to her values. She was passionate about her beliefs and never pretended to be anyone but herself. Perhaps that is why "Victorianism" has come to mean an entire code of behavior. Synonymous with conservative morality, the word comes from an era during which the monarchy finally represented virtuous leadership. Queen Victoria served as a role model for people throughout the world. Her life continues to set an example for future generations.

Notes

Introduction: An Anchor in Rough and Stormy Seas

1. Quoted in Giles St. Aubyn, *Queen Victoria: A Portrait*. London: Sinclair-Stevenson, 1991, p. 597.
2. Quoted in Stanley Weintraub, *Victoria*. New York: E.P. Dutton, 1988, p. 642.
3. Quoted in St. Aubyn, *Queen Victoria: A Portrait*, p. 597.
4. Quoted in John Van der Kiste, *Queen Victoria's Children*. Trowbridge, UK: Alan Sutton, 1990, p. 141.
5. Quoted in St. Aubyn, *Queen Victoria: A Portrait*, p. 597.
6. Quoted in Elizabeth Longford, *Victoria R.I.* London: Pan Books, 1983, p. 708.
7. Quoted in Weintraub, *Victoria*, p. 639.
8. Quoted in Longford, *Victoria R.I.*, p. 709.
9. Quoted in Longford, *Victoria R.I.*, p. 709.
10. Quoted in Longford, *Victoria R.I.*, p. 709.
11. Quoted in Longford, *Victoria R.I.*, p. 709.
12. Quoted in Weintraub, *Victoria*, p. 641.
13. Victor Mallet, ed., *Life with Queen Victoria—Marie Mallet's Letters from Court 1887–1901*. Boston: Houghton Mifflin, 1968, p. xi.
14. Quoted in Weintraub, *Victoria*, p. 643.

Chapter 1: An Unhappy Childhood

15. Quoted in St. Aubyn, *Queen Victoria: A Portrait*, p. 8.
16. Quoted in Monica Charlot, *Victoria: The Young Queen*. Oxford: Blackwell, 1991, p. 26.
17. Quoted in Cecil Woodham-Smith, *Queen Victoria: From Her Birth to the Death of the Prince Consort*. New York: Dell, 1972, p. 72.
18. Quoted in Weintraub, *Victoria*, p. 53.

19. Quoted in Woodham-Smith, *Queen Victoria: From Her Birth to the Death of the Prince Consort*, p. 73.
20. Quoted in St. Aubyn, *Queen Victoria: A Portrait*, pp. 16–17.
21. Quoted in Woodham-Smith, *Queen Victoria: From Her Birth to the Death of the Prince Consort*, p. 80.
22. Quoted in Woodham-Smith, *Queen Victoria: From Her Birth to the Death of the Prince Consort*, p. 71.
23. Quoted in Woodham-Smith, *Queen Victoria: From Her Birth to the Death of the Prince Consort*, p. 71.
24. Quoted in Weintraub, *Victoria*, p. 54.
25. Quoted in Weintraub, *Victoria*, p. 54.
26. Quoted in St. Aubyn, *Queen Victoria: A Portrait*, p. 14.
27. Quoted in St. Aubyn, *Queen Victoria: A Portrait*, p. 14.
28. Quoted in St. Aubyn, *Queen Victoria: A Portrait*, p. 15.
29. Quoted in Charlot, *Victoria: The Young Queen*, p. 52.
30. Quoted in Charlot, *Victoria: The Young Queen*, p. 45.

Chapter 2: The Power of the Throne

31. Weintraub, *Victoria*, p. 70.
32. St. Aubyn, *Queen Victoria: A Portrait*, p. 26.
33. Quoted in Weintraub, *Victoria*, p. 75.
34. Quoted in St. Aubyn, *Queen Victoria: A Portrait*, pp. 21–22.
35. Quoted in Woodham-Smith, *Queen Victoria: From Her Birth to the Death of the Prince Consort*, p. 123.

36. Quoted in Woodham-Smith, *Queen Victoria: From Her Birth to the Death of the Prince Consort*, pp. 121–122.

37. Quoted in Longford, *Victoria R.I.*, p. 52.

38. Quoted in St. Aubyn, *Queen Victoria: A Portrait*, p. 33.

39. Quoted in Charlot, *Victoria: The Young Queen*, p. 62.

40. Quoted in Charlot, *Victoria: The Young Queen*, p. 65.

41. Quoted in Charlot, *Victoria: The Young Queen*, p. 65.

42. Quoted in Woodham-Smith, *Queen Victoria: From Her Birth to the Death of the Prince Consort*, p. 133.

43. Quoted in Charlot, *Victoria: The Young Queen*, p. 128.

44. Quoted in Charlot, *Victoria: The Young Queen*, p. 64.

45. Quoted in Charlot, *Victoria: The Young Queen*, p. 65.

46. Quoted in Charlot, *Victoria: The Young Queen*, pp. 65–66.

47. Quoted in Woodham-Smith, *Queen Victoria: From Her Birth to the Death of the Prince Consort*, p. 141.

48. Quoted in Weintraub, *Victoria*, p. 81.

49. Quoted in Woodham-Smith, *Queen Victoria: From Her Birth to the Death of the Prince Consort*, p. 144.

50. Quoted in Charlot, *Victoria: The Young Queen*, p. 66.

51. Quoted in Weintraub, *Victoria*, p. 92.

52. Quoted in Charlot, *Victoria: The Young Queen*, p. 67.

53. Quoted in Weintraub, *Victoria*, p. 91.

54. Quoted in Weintraub, *Victoria*, p. 92.

55. Quoted in Longford, *Victoria R.I.*, p. 73.

56. Quoted in Woodham-Smith, *Queen Victoria: From Her Birth to the Death of the Prince Consort*, p. 182.

57. Quoted in Woodham-Smith, *Queen Victoria: From Her Birth to the Death of the Prince Consort*, p. 184.

58. Quoted in Woodham-Smith, *Queen Victoria: From Her Birth to the Death of the Prince Consort*, p. 184.

59. Quoted in Woodham-Smith, *Queen Victoria: From Her Birth to the Death of the Prince Consort*, p. 187.

60. Quoted in Longford, *Victoria R.I.*, p. 79.

Chapter 3: Advisors and Enemies

61. Quoted in Longford, *Victoria R.I.*, p. 80.

62. Quoted in Woodham-Smith, *Queen Victoria: From Her Birth to the Death of the Prince Consort*, p. 191.

63. Quoted in Woodham-Smith, *Queen Victoria: From Her Birth to the Death of the Prince Consort*, pp. 190–191.

64. Quoted in St. Aubyn, *Queen Victoria: A Portrait*, p. 68.

65. Quoted in Charlot, *Victoria: The Young Queen*, p. 92.

66. Quoted in Charlot, *Victoria: The Young Queen*, p. 93.

67. Quoted in Woodham-Smith, *Queen Victoria: From Her Birth to the Death of the Prince Consort*, pp. 186–187.

68. Quoted in Woodham-Smith, *Queen Victoria: From Her Birth to the Death of the Prince Consort*, p. 187.

69. Quoted in Woodham-Smith, *Queen Victoria: From Her Birth to the Death of the Prince Consort*, p. 187.

70. Quoted in Charlot, *Victoria: The Young Queen*, p. 101.

71. Quoted in Woodham-Smith, *Queen Victoria: From Her Birth to the Death of the Prince Consort*, p. 188.

72. Quoted in Longford, *Victoria R.I.*, p. 93.

73. Quoted in Weintraub, *Victoria*, pp. 112–113.

74. Quoted in St. Aubyn, *Queen Victoria: A Portrait*, p. 93.

75. Quoted in Longford, *Victoria R.I.*, p. 121.

76. Quoted in Charlot, *Victoria: The Young Queen*, p. 137.

77. Quoted in Charlot, *Victoria: The Young Queen*, p. 141.

78. Quoted in Christopher Hibbert, *Queen Victoria in Her Letters and Journals*. New York: Penguin, 1985, p. 49.

79. Quoted in Charlot, *Victoria: The Young Queen*, p. 150.

Chapter 4: A Royal Marriage

80. Quoted in Weintraub, *Victoria*, p. 89.

81. Quoted in Lytton Strachey, *Queen Victoria*. New York: Harcourt, Brace & World, 1921, p. 52.

82. Quoted in Hibbert, *Queen Victoria in Her Letters and Journals*, p. 42.

83. Quoted in Woodham-Smith, *Queen Victoria: From Her Birth to the Death of the Prince Consort*, p. 241.

84. Quoted in Woodham-Smith, *Queen Victoria: From Her Birth to the Death of the Prince Consort*, p. 242.

85. Quoted in Charlot, *Victoria: The Young Queen*, p. 168.

86. Quoted in Charlot, *Victoria: The Young Queen*, p. 168.

87. Quoted in Weintraub, *Victoria*, p. 133.

88. Quoted in Longford, *Victoria R.I.*, p. 170.

89. Quoted in St. Aubyn, *Queen Victoria: A Portrait*, p. 141.

90. Quoted in Woodham-Smith, *Queen Victoria: From Her Birth to the Death of the Prince Consort*, p. 263.

91. Quoted in Woodham-Smith, *Queen Victoria: From Her Birth to the Death of the Prince Consort*, p. 264.

92. Quoted in Hibbert, *Queen Victoria in Her Letters and Journals*, p. 61.

93. Quoted in St. Aubyn, *Queen Victoria: A Portrait*, p. 143.

94. Quoted in Weintraub, *Victoria*, p. 134.

95. Quoted in Strachey, *Queen Victoria*. pp. 152–153.

96. Quoted in Weintraub, *Victoria*, p. 135.

97. Quoted in St. Aubyn, *Queen Victoria: A Portrait*, p. 144.

98. Quoted in Longford, *Victoria R.I.*, p. 176.

99. Quoted in Charlot, *Victoria: The Young Queen*, p. 183.

100. Quoted in Charlot, *Victoria: The Young Queen*, p. 185.

101. Quoted in Woodham-Smith, *Queen Victoria: From Her Birth to the Death of the Prince Consort*, p. 269.

102. Quoted in Woodham-Smith, *Queen Victoria: From Her Birth to the Death of the Prince Consort*, p. 269.

103. Quoted in Woodham-Smith, *Queen Victoria: From Her Birth to the Death of the Prince Consort*, p. 270.

104. Quoted in Longford, *Victoria R.I.*, p. 184.

105. Quoted in Charlot, *Victoria: The Young Queen*, p. 190.

106. Quoted in Charlot, *Victoria: The Young Queen*, p. 190.

Chapter 5: Head of the Household

107. Quoted in Charlot, *Victoria: The Young Queen*, p. 191.

108. Quoted in St. Aubyn, *Queen Victoria: A Portrait*, p. 165.

109. Quoted in Van der Kiste, *Queen Victoria's Children*, p. 12.

110. Quoted in Longford, *Victoria R.I.*, p. 200.

111. Quoted in Longford, *Victoria R.I.*, p. 201.

112. Quoted in St. Aubyn, *Queen Victoria: A Portrait*, p. 172.

113. Quoted in St. Aubyn, *Queen Victoria: A Portrait*, p. 176.

114. Quoted in Van der Kiste, *Queen Victoria's Children*, p. 17.

115. Quoted in Charlot, *Victoria: The Young Queen*, p. 296.

116. Quoted in Charlot, *Victoria: The Young Queen*, p. 202.

Chapter 6: Political Decisions

117. Quoted in Weintraub, *Victoria*, p. 156.

118. Quoted in Strachey, *Queen Victoria*, p. 189.

119. Quoted in Weintraub, *Victoria*, p. 187.

120. Quoted in St. Aubyn, *Queen Victoria: A Portrait*, p. 244.

121. Quoted in St. Aubyn, *Queen Victoria: A Portrait*, p. 247.

122. Quoted in Charlot, *Victoria: The Young Queen*, p. 349.

123. Quoted in Strachey, *Queen Victoria*, p. 252.

124. Quoted in Charlot, *Victoria: The Young Queen*, p. 353.

125. Quoted in Longford, *Victoria R.I.*, p. 309.

Chapter 7: Problems and Progress

126. Quoted in St. Aubyn, *Queen Victoria: A Portrait*, p. 226.

127. Quoted in St. Aubyn, *Queen Victoria: A Portrait*, p. 354.

128. Quoted in Longford, *Victoria R.I.*, p. 441.

129. Quoted in St. Aubyn, *Queen Victoria: A Portrait*, p. 228.

130. Quoted in Charlot, *Victoria: The Young Queen*, p. 329.

131. Quoted in Weintraub, *Victoria*, p. 220.

132. Quoted in Woodham-Smith, *Queen Victoria: From Her Birth to the Death of the Prince Consort*, p. 496.

133. Quoted in Charlot, *Victoria: The Young Queen*, p. 374.

134. Quoted in Charlot, *Victoria: The Young Queen*, p. 385.

135. Quoted in Weintraub, *Victoria*, p. 274.

136. Quoted in Charlot, *Victoria: The Young Queen*, p. 399.

137. Quoted in Woodham-Smith, *Queen Victoria: From Her Birth to the Death of the Prince Consort*, p. 521.

Chapter 8: The Shadow of Grief

138. Quoted in Charlot, *Victoria: The Young Queen*, p. 408.

139. Quoted in Charlot, *Victoria: The Young Queen*, p. 408.

140. Quoted in St. Aubyn, *Queen Victoria: A Portrait*, p. 322.

141. Quoted in Woodham-Smith, *Queen Victoria: From Her Birth to the Death of the Prince Consort*, p. 529.

142. Quoted in Woodham-Smith, *Queen Victoria: From Her Birth to the Death of the Prince Consort*, p. 529–530.

143. Quoted in Charlot, *Victoria: The Young Queen*, p. 417.

144. Quoted in Woodham-Smith, *Queen Victoria: From Her Birth to the Death of the Prince Consort*, p. 536.

145. Quoted in Van der Kiste, *Queen Victoria's Children*, p. 41.

146. Quoted in Strachey, *Queen Victoria*, p. 295.

147. Quoted in Charlot, *Victoria: The Young Queen*, p. 420.

148. Quoted in Charlot, *Victoria: The Young Queen*, p. 424.

149. Quoted in Charlot, *Victoria: The Young Queen*, p. 424.

150. Quoted in Hibbert, *Queen Victoria in Her Letters and Journals*, p. 156.

151. Quoted in Woodham-Smith, *Queen Victoria: From Her Birth to the Death of the Prince Consort*, p. 553.

152. Quoted in Strachey, *Queen Victoria*, p. 303.

153. Quoted in Strachey, *Queen Victoria*, pp. 303–304.

154. Quoted in Weintraub, *Victoria*, p. 308.

155. Quoted in Van der Kiste, *Queen Victoria's Children*, p. 47.

156. Quoted in Weintraub, *Victoria*, p. 321.

157. Quoted in Weintraub, *Victoria*, p. 324.

Chapter 9: Ruling an Empire

158. Quoted in St. Aubyn, *Queen Victoria: A Portrait*, p. 399.

159. Quoted in Hibbert, *Queen Victoria in Her Letters and Journals*, p. 172.

160. Quoted in Weintraub, *Victoria*, p. 322.

161. Quoted in Weintraub, *Victoria*, p. 323.

162. Quoted in St. Aubyn, *Queen Victoria: A Portrait*, p. 344.

163. Quoted in Longford, *Victoria R.I.*, p. 401.

164. Quoted in St. Aubyn, *Queen Victoria: A Portrait*, p. 345.

165. Quoted in Longford, *Victoria R.I.*, p. 407.

166. Quoted in St. Aubyn, *Queen Victoria: A Portrait*, p. 356.

167. Quoted in St. Aubyn, *Queen Victoria: A Portrait*, p. 357.

168. Quoted in Dorothy Thompson, *Queen Victoria: Gender and Power*. London: Virago Press, 1990, p. 59.

169. Quoted in St. Aubyn, *Queen Victoria: A Portrait*, p. 360.

170. Quoted in Thompson, *Queen Victoria: Gender and Power*, p. 72.

171. Quoted in Longford, *Victoria R.I.*, p. 470.

172. Quoted in Weintraub, *Victoria*, p. 347.

173. Quoted in Longford, *Victoria R.I.*, p. 458.

174. Quoted in Weintraub, *Victoria*, pp. 351–352.

175. Quoted in Weintraub, *Victoria*, p. 352.

176. Quoted in Weintraub, *Victoria*, p. 360.

177. Quoted in Weintraub, *Victoria*, p. 363.

178. Quoted in Weintraub, *Victoria*, p. 368.

Chapter 10: Beloved Queen

179. Quoted in Longford, *Victoria R.I.*, p. 505.

180. Quoted in St. Aubyn, *Queen Victoria: A Portrait*, p. 219.

181. Quoted in Longford, *Victoria R.I.*, p. 466.

182. Quoted in Longford, *Victoria R.I.*, p. 466.

183. Quoted in Longford, *Victoria R.I.*, pp. 495–496.

184. Quoted in St. Aubyn, *Queen Victoria: A Portrait*, p. 484.

185. Quoted in St. Aubyn, *Queen Victoria: A Portrait*, p. 483.

186. Quoted in Longford, *Victoria R.I.*, p. 504.

187. Quoted in St. Aubyn, *Queen Victoria: A Portrait*, pp. 376–377.

188. Quoted in Strachey, *Queen Victoria*, p. 346.

189. Quoted in St. Aubyn, *Queen Victoria: A Portrait*, p. 377.

190. Quoted in St. Aubyn, *Queen Victoria: A Portrait*, p. 378.

191. Quoted in Weintraub, *Victoria*, p. 442.

192. Quoted in Weintraub, *Victoria*, p. 444.

193. Quoted in Strachey, *Queen Victoria*, p. 336.

194. Quoted in Thompson, *Queen Victoria: Gender and Power*, p. 121.

195. Quoted in Longford, *Victoria*, p. 682.

196. Quoted in Longford, *Victoria*, p. 673.

197. Quoted in Thompson, *Queen Victoria: Gender and Power*, p. 124.

198. Quoted in Thompson, *Queen Victoria: Gender and Power*, p. 133.

199. Quoted in Thompson, *Queen Victoria: Gender and Power*, p. 135.

200. St. Aubyn, *Queen Victoria: A Portrait*, p. 546.

201. Quoted in St. Aubyn, *Queen Victoria: A Portrait*, pp. 547–548.

202. Quoted in Hibbert, *Queen Victoria in Her Letters and Journals*, p. 246.

203. Quoted in Hibbert, *Queen Victoria in Her Letters and Journals*, p. 301.

204. Quoted in St. Aubyn, *Queen Victoria: A Portrait*, p. 605.

205. St. Aubyn, *Queen Victoria: A Portrait*, pp. 606–607.

206. Quoted in Mallet, *Life with Queen Victoria*, p. 37.

207. Quoted in St. Aubyn, *Queen Victoria: A Portrait*, p. 594.

208. Quoted in Weintraub, *Victoria*, p. 635.

209. Quoted in St. Aubyn, *Queen Victoria: A Portrait*, p. 596.

210. Quoted in Longford, *Victoria R.I.*, p. 726.

211. Longford, *Victoria R.I.*, p. 726.

212. Sir Edgar Trevor Williams and Meredith Veldman, "Victoria and the Victorian Age," in *The New Encyclopaedia Britannica Macropaedia*, vol. 29. Chicago: Encyclopaedia Britannica, 1994, p. 492.

213. Williams and Veldman, "Victoria and the Victorian Age," p. 492.

For Further Reading

David Evans, *How We Used to Live: Victorians Early & Late.* New York: Talman, 1991. This book offers an overview of the Victorian era.

Manuel Komroff, *Disraeli.* New York: J. Messner, 1963. This biography describes the life of Victoria's favorite prime minister.

Michael Rawcliffe, *Finding Out About: Life in Edwardian Britain.* Trafalgar, UK: Batsford, 1989. This little book tells about England during the reign of Victoria's eldest son, Edward VII.

Dierdre Shearman, *Queen Victoria.* New Haven, CT: Chelsea House, 1986. This excellent biography offers many fine illustrations and photographs.

Noel Streatfeild, *Queen Victoria.* New York: Random House, 1958. This well-written book is a classic biography for young people.

Richard Tames, *Radicals, Reformers, and Railways 1815–1851.* Trafalgar, UK: Batsford, 1987. This book talks about some of the changes that took place during the Victorian era.

Marina Warner, *Queen Victoria's Sketchbook.* New York: Crown Publishers, 1979. This book features Victoria's own drawings.

Lesley Young, *Queen Victoria.* Trafalgar, UK: Evans Bros. Ltd., 1991. This book is another fine biography for young people.

Works Consulted

Monica Charlot, *Victoria: The Young Queen.* Oxford: Blackwell, 1991. This well-written book chronicles Victoria's life up until the death of her husband.

Christopher Hibbert, *Queen Victoria in Her Letters and Journals.* New York: Penguin, 1985. This biography uses excerpts from the queen's letters and journals to tell the story of her life.

Elizabeth Longford, *Victoria R.I.* London: Pan Books, 1983. Though more difficult reading, this book is one of the most important and complete biographies of Queen Victoria.

Victor Mallet, ed., *Life with Queen Victoria—Marie Mallet's Letters from Court 1887–1901.* Boston: Houghton Mifflin, 1968. This book of letters written by Victoria's lady-in-waiting offers an entertaining perspective on life in the queen's court.

Giles St. Aubyn, *Queen Victoria: A Portrait.* London: Sinclair-Stevenson, 1991. Though difficult reading, this book is a very thorough and informative biography of the queen.

Barry St. John Nevill, ed., *Life at the Court of Queen Victoria, 1861–1901.* Exeter, England: Webb and Bower, 1984. This highly visual book illustrates selections from the queen's journals with pictures from the scrapbooks of Lord Edward Pelham-Clinton, who was in the queen's household.

Lytton Strachey, *Queen Victoria.* New York: Harcourt, Brace & World, 1921. This is one of the earliest biographies of Queen Victoria.

Dorothy Thompson, *Queen Victoria: Gender and Power.* London: Virago Press, 1990. This valuable book offers not only a biography of the queen but a collection of poems, cartoons, and illustrations from the Victorian period.

John Van der Kiste, *Queen Victoria's Children.* Trowbridge, UK: Alan Sutton, 1990. This concise guide has many photographs of the royal family, along with charts explaining exactly how family members were related.

Stanley Weintraub, *Victoria.* New York: E.P. Dutton, 1988. This book is quite long, but also very entertaining.

Sir Edgar Trevor Williams and Meredith Veldman, "Victoria and the Victorian Age," in *The New Encyclopaedia Britannica Macropaedia.* Vol. 29. Chicago: Encyclopaedia Britannica, 1994. This scholarly article offers both fact and analysis on Victoria's entire reign.

Cecil Woodham-Smith, *Queen Victoria: From Her Birth to the Death of the Prince Consort.* New York: Knopf, 1972. This highly detailed book quotes from many of the queen's writings.

Index

Picture Credits

Cover photo: FPG International

The Bettmann Archive, 22, 27, 33, 43, 65, 69, 71, 75, 76, 77, 79, 87, 89, 91, 92, 95, 101, 105, 106, 112

Library of Congress, 12

The Royal Collection © Her Majesty the Queen Elizabeth II, 24, 45, 49

UPI/Bettmann Newsphotos, 11, 16, 63, 104

About the Author

Patricia D. Netzley received a bachelor's degree in English from the University of California at Los Angeles (UCLA). After graduation she worked as an editor at the UCLA Medical Center, where she produced hundreds of medical articles, speeches, and pamphlets.

Netzley became a freelance writer in 1986. She is the author of three other books for young people, *The Assassination of President John F. Kennedy* (Macmillan/New Discovery Books, 1994), *Alien Abductions* (Greenhaven Press, 1996), and *The Mysterious Death of Butch Cassidy* (Lucent Books, 1997).

Netzley is also an accomplished needleworker. Her favorite pastime is weaving on a four-harness floor loom. She and her husband Ray live in Southern California with their three children, Matthew, Sarah, and Jacob.